Crypto Technical Analysis

ALAN JOHN AND JON LAW

Jon Law, 2021

ISBN 9798527837636

Contact jonlawpublishing@gmail.com or alanjohnpublishing@gmail.com for further information regarding copyright, fair use, or this disclaimer.

Notes:

All charts in this book are real and handpicked.

All charts were created with TradingView. Credit to TradingView is provided in per-image footnotes and endnotes. All images are original unless otherwise noted.

All website links are correct as of 2021 and may be out of date.

The authors and invested parties are not endorsed or affiliated by any service, website, or business mentioned in this book.

TABLE OF CONTENTS; AT A GLANCE

TABLE OF CONTENTS: EXPANDED

ABOUT THIS BOOK

This project has consumed an enormous amount of time. It has filled many late nights and early mornings, and now, nearing the end of it, I can say I've had an incredible ride. I think cryptocurrency truly does have the potential to change the landscape of finance around the world, as well as the greater horizon of daily life for all people, and for that reason, I'm dedicating two years of my life to writing books on everything cryptocurrency: technical analysis, a crypto dictionary, crypto for beginners, blockchain, and much more. This book, especially, is truly valuable because it explores a valuable (not to mention wacky, when you think about it) skill: the ability to turn numbers, lines, and graphs on a screen into real-world profit. It's a life-changer, and I hope you see that as I do.

To end off this end to the beginning (for me, as I write this, more like the beginning of the end) I must give a big thank you to you; this book was created for a person such as yourself, and I'm glad it's reached you. Now, let's get to it, and I'm pleased to introduce to you: *Crypto Technical Analysis: The Guide.*

HOW TO USE THIS BOOK

As I write this, I'm assuming several things about you:

A.   You know what Bitcoin and Altcoins are.

B.   You know what Blockchain is (as much as anyone can).

C.   You are very, very excited to get started (100% required!).

If you know those three things, you're free to continue. Everything else, as far as analysis goes, is covered. If you don't know any of these things, I suggest that you take a moment to learn about them and, if you wish, consult the essential terms dictionary in the resources section at the back of this book and the bonus section (in the back matter) about blockchain. If you do have this base layer of knowledge, great! We cover the rest.

The book is split into the following "macro" sections:

Part 1: Crypto Analysis

Part 2: Technical Analysis

Part 1 will provide a brief but complete introduction to the trading and analysis of cryptocurrencies and covers an introduction to technical analysis, fundamental analysis, and hype analysis, "the key three," types of indicators, white papers, the Big-Brother technique, supply mechanisms, burning, and more.

Part 2 will provide the reference portion of the subject matter of this book, namely, it's all about technical analysis. We'll dive into charts, patterns, oscillators, and other indicators, and then we'll tie it all off with crypto trading rules, algorithmic trading, trading biases, and more.

Following Part 2, the resource section provides a base to learn more about crypto. This includes glossaries, YouTube channels, podcasts, books, the bonus section, and more. I suggest that you take full advantage of the resources section and read both sections (especially Part 1) in sequential order. That said, much of the content in Part 2 can, and should, be referred to and searched back upon as wished.

That's it in terms of how to use this book; I do hope that it's fairly straightforward. However, while you may know how to use this book, I have not yet covered how not to use this book!

HOW NOT TO USE THIS BOOK

After you read this book, please don't immediately do the following:

A.   Invest all your money.

B.   Quit your job.

C.   Put all your money into Dogecoin.

On a real note, this book is meant to serve as an introductory guide and reference tool. It's meant to fully prepare you to enter the world of trading. To master that world, you need to be willing to learn and stick with it, whether as a weekend hobbyist or a full-time trader. So, take your time, enjoy the process, and don't put all your money into Dogecoin (yet).

PART 1: CRYPTO ANALYSIS

CRYPTO ANALYSIS

As mentioned, this part will contain a complete introduction to analysis. Following this section, you'll be able to confidently research coins or tokens in order to make educated trading decisions. Subsequently, part 2 dives into technical analysis. I've organized the parts as such because the whole of analysis is a necessary requirement to advance into technical analysis. We'll begin with the topic of myths.

MYTH-BUSTING

Crypto, I must say, has been blown up beyond proportion in terms of the risk vs. reward dynamic. Yes, the rewards are immense, but the market won't always be easy money, and the risk matches the reward. I'd like to start this off with a dose of reality, not to point out that the dream of crypto isn't real, but to point out that the dream takes effort. If that effort is put in, the rewards can change your life. If the effort isn't put in, risk will make itself blatantly known.

EASY MONEY

If you're reading this around the time of this writing in early 2021, the crypto market is in a massive bull run. Over the past six months, any investor could put money in any well-known coin and turned a profit. However, as I elaborate upon in rule #1 (later, in the cryptocurrency trading rules), this situation cannot last. It may take one month, six months, a year, or beyond. Whatever the case, making money in the cryptocurrency market won't always be easy, just like it is not easy to make money in stocks, real estate, options, or derivatives. Even if it is easy to make money in the market *right now*, operating from such a mindset can only lead to failure. You can save yourself this learning curve by maintaining strong trading principles, obeying the rules outlined later in this section, doing your research, thinking as rationally and unemotionally as possible, and using historical data to back up your decisions.

RISK-FREE

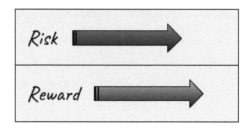

Figure 1: Risk vs. Reward [i]

Consider this picture. It is based on a principle called the risk-return tradeoff (to be later examined in the risk versus reward section). When one sees everyone else making money (or at least, social media would lead us to believe that everyone is making money), as is currently happening in the crypto market, we're prone to think that it is not very risky. If everyone's making money, how can it be risky? The risk-return tradeoff principle answers this. Generally speaking (you can surely think of examples that defy this, but exceptions only prove the rule), the more reward there is, the more risk there is. So, investing in cryptocurrencies is not risk-free. It is not low risk. It is extremely risky and offers extreme reward and should be treated as such.

100% ACCURATE

This myth applies specifically to technical analysis. Technical Analysis is a bet on probability; if something has happened more than 50% of the time in the past, given similar conditions to a current event, it is likely to happen again. Perhaps the probability is 60%, 80%, or 100%. In any case, technical analysts bet on the occurrence of historical patterns. Unfortunately, due to the fundamental nature of probability and trading, nothing is ever really certain to happen. Even if all your signals line up, the move that you think will happen may not happen. Really though, this can be freeing! It is completely fine to be wrong, and just because your strategy didn't work a few times doesn't mean it won't work over time. If it is a strategy that has historically proven to be profitable, it probably will be. In this way, it works both for you and against you: nothing will work all the time, but many things should work most of the time. So, rely on data, always adjust and improve, and learn to be comfortable with things not working out, no matter how much you think they should go right.

THE TWO TYPES OF CRYPTO ANALYSIS

Two umbrella methodologies of analysis exist: [1] technical analysis and fundamental analysis. You bought this book to learn about technical analysis; we will start off by filling in all the holes. A complete introduction to technical analysis is followed by fundamental analysis, and finally a third type of analysis. We will then cover some basic analysis metrics that can be used alongside all types of analysis. If you've been in the space for a little while, you'll probably already know some of this, but I'd also bet there's a lot you could learn, and for that reason, I suggest you read on. And, if you aren't yet an intermediate to advanced trader, this will get you well on your way.

---

[1] We'll stick with this for the sake of simplicity. There are more than just these two, depending on your perspective.

TECHNICAL ANALYSIS

Technical analysis is the discipline by which future movements of securities, currency pairs, and cryptocurrencies are discerned from historical patterns. Simply put, technical analysis is using history to figure out the future. History, in turn, is analyzed through the spectrum of patterns and indicators within charts. While on the topic of history, technical analysis has a long one; the core principles were first put into practice by a Dutch trader named Joseph de la Vega in the 17th century. Within a similar time period, traders in Japan's rice futures markets developed similar ideas. Early writing into behavioral economics, trends, and the invention of the candlestick chart can also be attributed to Japan and rice futures markets. Forms of technical analysis could also be found in text dating back to Imperial China and ancient Babylon. In more recent history, modern technical analysis is due, in large part, to Charles Dow.[2] Many of his ideas and those of others expanded into a developed and mainstream form of analysis by the mid-to-late 20th century.

THE KEY THREE

Now that you have some idea of what technical analysis is, you need to equip your technical (no pun intended) definition with a ideology-driven base that forms the logic by which technical analysts trade. We will do this through the key three. The key three are a collection of popularized statements (as an academic would say, "premises") that dictate the reasoning behind technical analysis. Practically everything related to technical analysis, such as indicators, analyzing charts, and even the entire basis of buying and selling assets based on historical events, is based upon these statements. We will begin with #1.

---

[2] After whom the Dow Jones Index was partly named.

HISTORY TENDS TO REPEAT ITSELF

While the idea that history tends to repeat itself may sound self-explanatory, it is actually quite a novel concept. Consider the question: Why should history repeat itself (history purely in relation to investments)? There aren't any rules that require the prices of investments to act a certain way, and there's no inherent intelligence to dictate historical movement in relation to current and future movement. However, the entire basis of technical analysis is that history does repeat itself, since if history repeats itself, history can be predicted, and if history can be predicted, money can be made. So, assuming the above, tendencies to repeat events must be due to outside influences, namely, the investors themselves. Much of this can be traced back to investor psychology (much of which will be discussed further in the book) and self-predicting patterns, while much of the rest is due to institutional investment. Whatever the reasoning, if you're looking to be successful at technical analysis, you better believe in the fact that history repeats itself.

THE MARKET DISCOUNTS EVERYTHING

The idea that the market discounts everything, often phrased as "market action discounts everything," is a part of an Efficient Market Hypothesis (EMH). The EMH states that prices (within our context, the prices of cryptocurrencies) reflect all available information. Various versions of this theory exist, which are thought of as weak, strong, and everything in-between. For example, since the crypto market is highly volatile and somewhat more trend-based than other security markets, it may be less of an efficient market because prices and price increases may not accurately reflect true value. For example, if Elon Musk tweets about a small-cap crypto and the price trends 500% up, it is arguable that the price increase did not represent an efficient market because the true value of the project didn't change. However, the idea that the market isn't completely efficient is a great thing because that opens up the availability of undervalued projects. Technical analysis, in part, aims to identify discounted prices through technical means. However, circling back to the original statement, the idea that the market discounts everything means that most future action is already reflected in the current price. For example, if company X is expected to launch an app in 30 days, the current price already reflects this information even though it hasn't happened yet. Assuming this phenomenon on a wider scale, it is logical to assume that the only real analysis that matters is the analysis of the price action since random variables such as announcements cannot be accounted for in advance. So, technical analysts care more about what is most likely to happen given historical events than what may happen based on information already priced into the security (such as trading based on earnings, trends, hype, etc.). This trading style can also be self-fulfilling because, in a certain way, traders create the things they believe will happen by trading as if those things will happen.

PRICES MOVE IN TRENDS

Trends are an exceedingly important concept to technical analysts. A technical analyst must accept the idea that markets and prices trend because, otherwise, the entire point of charting price movements is rendered illegitimate. So, one must assume that prices move in trends and that trends are more likely to continue than reverse.

SUMMARY

As an technical trader, one must believe that history repeats itself, the market discounts everything, and prices move in trends. These three statements form the ideological basis on which all technical analysis is based.

TYPES OF INDICATORS

To finish off our introduction to technical analysis, we will take a look at different types of indicators used in the field. Each will be expanded upon in great detail later in the book; this section merely serves as an introduction, albeit an important one.

CHART PATTERNS

Many indicators are patterns on charts. Charts, in turn, are just prices moving up and down, which is price action. Price action that behaves in a predictable way is a pattern, and patterns can be traded upon as a reliable indicator.

LEADING VS. LAGGING

Indicators are either "leading" or "lagging." Leading indicators predict future price movement, while lagging indicators provide signals once price action has already begun or happened. Leading indicators typically react quickly but are less accurate than the alternative, while lagging indicators are more accurate but may be late to the party. Typically, both types of indicators are combined, one (leading) to enter a position and the second (lagging) to confirm the entry.

SUPPORT AND RESISTANCE LEVELS

Support and resistance levels are probably the most commonly known chart-reading tool; you've likely heard of them, if not used them. Support and resistance levels indicate concentrated areas of buying or selling. At support levels, downtrends often pause due to a concentration of buyers, while resistance levels often stop uptrends due to a large concentration of sellers. Prices typically bounce between support and resistance levels before breaking out, either above resistance levels or below support levels. Then, a resistance level often become the new support level (for example, if Bitcoin breaks above resistance at 50k to 53k, 50k may become the new support), or support levels replace resistance levels.

Resistance levels are also sometimes referred to as "ceilings" and support levels as "floors." Here's a look at the support and resistance levels on Bitcoin:

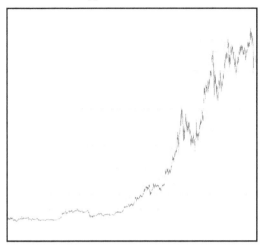

(tradingview.com) Figure 2: Support and Resistance[ii]

As you can see, the price tends to trade sideways along support and resistance levels. Then, a breakout occurs (as indicated with the arrows), new support and resistance levels are established, and the cycle restarts. Like all indicators, it isn't an exact science; however, support and resistance levels undeniably provide a basis for a large percentage of price movements and breakouts.

VOLUME AND MOMENTUM INDICATORS

Volume indicators provide insight into the number of trades combined with other factors, such as price (volume alone doesn't provide much insight as an indicator, hence why they're usually combined). Momentum indicators, on the other hand, measure the rate of change. Rate of change, in turn, helps determine strength or weakness in a price relative to history. So, momentum indicators show how fast prices move up and down, how strong or weak those movements are, and therefore how likely they are to continue. Popular volume and momentum indicators include the average directional index (ADX), rate of change (ROC), OBV Indicator, and volume RSI.

OSCILLATORS

Oscillators are indicators that vary within an upper limit and a lower limit (for example, between 0 and 100) and fluctuate within these limits. Oscillators work within very short timeframes and are used to discover overbought (sell) or oversold (buy) conditions. When the value of an oscillator is closer to an upper limit, it typically means that the asset is overbought, while the lower limit represents oversold conditions. Popular oscillators include the moving average convergence/divergence (MACD), relative strength index (RSI), money flow (MFI), and rate of change (ROC). The MACD, RSI, MFI, ROC, and others will all be thoroughly broken down later, as oscillators rank among the most important and most common types of indicators.

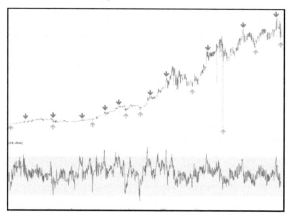

(tradingview.com) Figure 3: Oscillator Example[iii]

This is the RSI. Note the action in the bottom section, and to the right, you can see the number, followed by a line, vary within a range of 0 and 100. The number generally falls within the purple range, so between 30 and 70. Anytime it hits above 70, the coin is overbought and will likely pull back. This is a sell signal. A buy signal is indicated when it goes below 30. However, since this RSI rarely falls below 30, one may revise a buy signal to be, say, 40 or below, which is relatively low and thus indicates a strong relative overbought condition.

MOVING AVERAGE INDICATORS

Moving averages are lagging indicators that identify support levels, resistance levels, and trend direction. MAs smooth over data into singular lines. If the line is sloping upwards, it represents an uptrend, and if it is sloping downwards, it represents a downtrend. These lines then function as future support and resistance levels. Moving averages are calculated within a customizable time frame. The most popular time frames are 5, 10, 15, 20, 50, 100, and 200 days (for example, one may say they're looking at the "50-day moving average"). Different time frames can be used in conjunction; such crossings signify either a bullish or bearish move (bullish if the shorter-term MA crosses above the longer-term MA and bearish if the shorter-term MA falls below the longer-term MA). The two most popular moving averages are the simple moving average (SMA) and the exponential moving average (EMA).

(tradingview.com) Figure 4: Moving Average Indicator Example[iv]
*buy signals are in green thumbs-up symbols, sell signals in red.

Here, the 50-day MA and the 200-day MA are shown. Since the 50-day MA is short-term, it is more aligned with the price, while the 200-day MA is "smoother" and portrays more general trends as opposed to smaller-scale movements. Trading on MAs between the first "buy" signal and the first "sell" signal would result in a 2x gain, then re-entering at the second "buy" signal and selling at the second "sell" would result in a 5x gain. The resulting gain by trading on all the buy and sell signals would be a 13x, while simply holding would be a 10x. So, an active trader would be roughly 30% more profitable by using moving averages (in this case) than someone simply holding. While this is by no means the rule, it does nicely display the benefit that basic technical analysis and moving averages can bring.

VOLATILITY INDICATORS

Volatility indicators don't measure or predict trends. Rather, they measure risk, and risk provides a base layer of context about a coin or token (more on volatility is coming in the basic analysis section). Popular volatility indicators are standard deviations, the average true range (ATR), and Bollinger Bands.

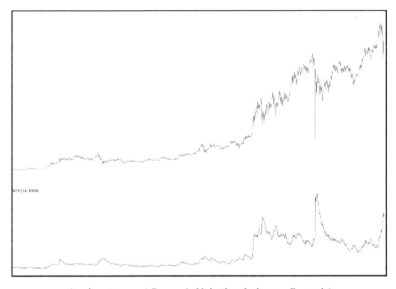

(tradingview.com) Figure 5: Volatility Indicator Example[v]

BEHAVIORAL TRADING

Technical analysts place a significant degree of importance on the psychological and behavioral aspects of prices. In this sense, behavioral instincts and psychology are an indicator (in the broader sense of the word) since they (from a technical analyst's perspective) affect prices. For example, Bitcoin probably has strong resistance at $50,000, and much of this resistance may come from the fact that $50,000 is a nice, round number that people place buy orders at. Through situations such as these and others, psychology is a viable part of price action and, hence, analysis. Check out the chart below to see the effect psychology has on trading:

(tradingview.com) Figure 6: Behavioral Trading Bitcoin Example[vii]

The above Bitcoin chart shows that most support and resistance levels are very near nice, round numbers, such as $30,000, $40,000, and $65,000. This also shows that this isn't the rule 100% of the time, as with $58,000 and $43,000. However, exceptions only prove the rule, and the rule is that numbers over which psychology holds more sway are often influence prices.

TECHNICAL ANALYSIS INTRODUCTION: COMPLETED!

In combination, all of the above indicators aim to alert (a trader about a trend), predict (future prices), and confirm (the prediction through other indicators). This three-step system from Jeff Desjardins of the *Visual Capitalist* very nicely simplifies the process. So, remember that the process by which trades are made and the purpose of indicators are to alert, predict, and confirm. That now sums up our introduction to technical analysis. Later in the book is a deep dive into technical analysis; for now we'll take a look at the other mainstream form of analysis.

FUNDAMENTAL ANALYSIS

Fundamental analysis revolves around analyzing the true value of an asset through valuation techniques that include overall economic analysis, industry and sector analysis, and analysis of a company's financial data. Since fundamental analysis relies purely on publicly available data, investors can find investments through either a top-down or bottom-up approach. In a top-down approach, the health and direction of the economy are first considered, then each sector, then each company. Investors select the best of each stage and funnel down to find undervalued opportunities. While this approach only works within the stock market (since the market covers all the industries and sectors of the economy), this same concept can be applied to top-down crypto fundamental analysis. Investors can first research the overall health of the crypto market, then identify a specific segment that they believe is undervalued. From there, the most undervalued companies and projects can be sought out. For example: I think the market will do well based on the data I've looked at. I think that crypto companies in the virtual reality space will do well since I believe the entire space is undervalued relative to short-term and long-term potential. I've looked at all the companies meeting the above criteria, and, upon further research, the most undervalued company appears to be Decentraland (MANA).

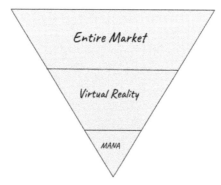

Figure 7: Top-Down Analysis

In this way, a top-down analysis can be performed. However, given the nature of the process, it requires a lot of time spent sorting through all sorts of data, first for the overall market, then through various sectors, and then through all the ongoing currencies in that sector. The opposite approach, bottom-up, first analyzes individual assets. This works because, in the stock market, individual stocks can easily outperform the overall industry or sector. Within the crypto space, I'd translate this to be the same, just magnified to a higher risk/reward ratio. So, how exactly does one analyze fundamental value?

First, I want to really explain the core idea of fundamental analysis, which is that coins have an intrinsic value that should be reflected in the price and that, to some degree, this intrinsic value should eventually be settled upon. Therefore, one can conclude that any price under this true value (remember, true value can change as new information comes out) renders it undervalued, and any price over the intrinsic value renders it overbought and a sell. Although the concept of value and identifying value may sound like an exact science (e.g., the true value of this crypto is $20 and it is trading at $15, time to make $5!), fundamental analysis is often quite speculative since people can have different opinions on what a given asset's true value should be. The central idea is that all stock or crypto investments are either undervalued or overvalued, and your job as a fundamental analyst is to find the most undervalued.

Fundamental analysts conduct research through a wide-ranging multitude of sources, but most information can be assembled through the following channels: on-chain metrics, project metrics, sentiment, utility, and relative value (quick note: the metric separation can be attributed to Binance Academy—full credit to them with that). While this list may sound lengthy, a full explanation of nearly everything above is covered in the basic analysis section shortly ahead. Take a look at the table of contents if you'd like to get an idea of what's discussed. So, I won't delve deep into the mentioned topics; all the basics are covered later and should provide a platform for further learning, of which there is plenty. For the moment, I'll just briefly describe each in relation to fundamental value. I also want to highlight that fundamental analysis is often used in conjunction with technical analysis: the pair can be used first to determine whether to buy into a market or coin (through FA) and then to identify good entry and exit levels (through TA).

ON-CHAIN METRICS

On-chain metrics are data about the network behind a coin. Basically, it's technical jargon, however it is very important jargon, and metrics such as average exchange deposits, miner deposits sent to exchanges, transaction amount and value, activity and value of addresses, hash rates, fees, and so on, are all very applicable in helping you arrive at investment decisions. That said, on-chain metrics are typically better for short-to-mid-term investments, as opposed to long-term and fundamental trading, since many of the mentioned metrics can change based on a variety of factors, such as through alterations in usage or various scaling solutions (such as Ethereum version 1 to Ethereum version 2).

PROJECT METRICS

Project metrics describe the big-picture and human elements of a cryptocurrency. This involves the team, white paper, events, and so on. This will be covered shortly.

SENTIMENT

Sentiment describes how people feel towards a given project. While a full explanation and sentiment resources are coming up, keep in mind that peoples' perception of value alters the value; hence, sentiment affects how undervalued or overvalued a coin or token is, and, therefore, sentiment is a part of fundamental value.

UTILITY

Utility is how useful a coin or token is and what real-world, practical application it has. Utility, like relative value (below), could be lumped into project metrics. However, the concept of utility is really valuable since the coins that win in the long term are the ones that are actually useful and, in some way, solve a problem and hence create utility.

RELATIVE VALUE

Relative value can technically be lumped in with project metrics, but given its importance, I feel that it should have a dedicated section. Relative value is analyzing either the true value and/or current value (basically, what you think it should be at versus what it is at) of competitors and comparing that to the coin or token you're looking into. For example, if you've done your research and concluded that 6 out of 14 virtual-reality crypto companies have experienced massive, 200% moons and MANA hasn't (please refer to the earlier example on page 30), then you must ask yourself why this hasn't happened. Perhaps something is wrong with the company, and MANA isn't a buy, or perhaps it just hasn't happened *yet,* and therefore MANA is an extremely undervalued buy. In this way, analyzing all sorts of metrics relative to similar projects is a great way to gauge value.

This concludes our brief breakdown of fundamental analysis. While this book is about technical analysis and technical analysis certainly is a profitable and much more adrenaline-inducing trading method, I believe that the best long-term strategies and portfolios employ multiple types of analysis, and fundamental analysis should certainly not be overlooked in terms of its reliability and widespread use.

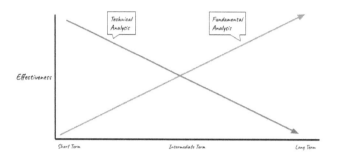

Figure 8: TA vs. FA Effectiveness Comparison

I'd like to make one more point before moving on using the chart above.[3] Generally, the effectiveness and correctness of technical analysis decreases with time, while the correctness of fundamental analysis increases over time. While it isn't a linear relationship as portrayed on the graph, this rule does hold true most of the time. Technical analysts usually aren't looking at indicators and deciding whether or not to hold a coin or token for months or years, while fundamental analysts aren't looking at market data to determine whether or not to buy a coin for a quick flip. By no means does this mean you should put yourself in a box; it just portrays the general difference in time frame between TA and FA and hence provides some context on the trading strategy you may choose.

---

[3] Inspiration for this visual from trading-education.com.

HYPE ANALYSIS

Hype analysis is not a commonly used term in the wider crypto world as I define it (technically, it could be categorized as part of the fundamental analysis), but it is the term I have chosen to describe the phenomenon that is analyzing real-world "hype" trends. Perhaps to a greater extent than any other sizable investment vehicles, the crypto market is driven by hype and trends. Elon Musk may be the wackiest example of this, since his tweets about cryptocurrencies are known to massively influence the price of the subject, whether positively or negatively. For example, Musk once tweeted just the word "Doge," and the price of Dogecoin (DOGE) proceeded to move from $0.036 to $0.082 in the following 5 days, a 220% gain. While this is mostly unfounded, subcategories within the crypto market, such as DeFi, FinTech, Gaming Coins, Web 3.0, and numerous others, often blow up all at once and cause most of the coins within the given area to experience massive, positive surges. In this way, and others, trading on trends and hype is a strategy that, historically speaking, is sound. While I don't necessarily advise this, and I'll explain why shortly, if it is done right, you can experience absolutely massive results. However, you are much more likely to do it wrong than to do it right, and I'd like to take a moment to elaborate upon the risk versus reward of all types of analysis, as well as provide a general introduction to risk versus reward and specifically identify the risk level this type of analysis.

RISK VERSUS REWARD

The concept of risk versus reward is the foundation of all investment decisions because an investor expects certain things from certain investments and chooses between, say, Bitcoin, stocks, and real estate as a result. A principle called the "risk-return tradeoff" dictates that higher risk is generally associated with higher reward. Let's revisit this visual from our myth-busting section a few pages back:

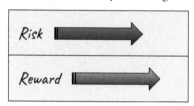

Figure 9: Risk vs. Reward #2

Risk is often measured from historical volatility. For example, government bonds, which have historically proven to carry very low risk, very little volatility, and insured investments. Then, take a penny stock. Let's go with CytoDyn, (OTCMKTS: CYDY), which has gone from $2.80 to $8.77, back to $2.02, up to $7, down to $2, and up to $4. All in the past year. In this way, since the volatility is much greater, the risk is much greater. However, despite the risk being greater, any investor who just held the stock would be up 10% for the year, a decent return, and any traders who sold at the right time would be up more than 100%. In this way, as per the mentioned principle, the risk equates to the reward. Of course, higher risk does not always equal higher return, and strategies can be taken to minimize risk within risky investments.

The cryptocurrency space is known as one of the—if not the single—riskiest investments. Despite the risk (and therefore the volatility), anyone who simply bought and held practically any major coin over the past few years is probably up several hundred percent, if not more than a thousand percent. So, while the crypto market is risky and volatile, the rewards can equate and exceed the risk. Let's put the magnifying glass of risk versus reward over the three types of analysis: technical analysis, fundamental analysis, and hype analysis.

Generally, fundamental analysis is used to determine the long-term value of a given investment, while technical analysis is used to determine short(er)-term investments. Fundamental analysis, in concept, carriers more unknown than technical analysis because technical analysis is based on absolutes in historical trading data, while fundamental analysis aims to identify overbought/oversold conditions that can change quickly and base themselves on subjective viewing to actually make the move that, fundamentally, the price should make. So, fundamental analysis is more theoretical than technical analysis, though with that being said, the spread of returns (for example, trader #1 makes 10%, trader #2 makes 50%, and trader #3 loses 60%) do not correlate all, or even much, of the time. So, learn about both strategies within the crypto space and beyond, and try different forms of each out for yourself. This, in the long-term, will allow you to *(tradingview.com)* Figure out what you prefer and what generates you the highest returns.

The third type of analysis, hype analysis, is much more volatile and riskier than the other two, and it is not a generally accepted nor a historically proven method of trading. However, in regard to the current market conditions within the crypto space, the rewards have outpaced the risks if proper research is done and safety protocols are put in place. Given the volatile and risky nature of attempting to analyze and trade upon trends, I suggest (most others would as well) that you start out with technical analysis, as described in this book, as well as some degree of fundamental analysis. Once you have some experience or in any other way feel comfortable to invest based on pure, trend-based speculation, here's how you to do it right. Please skip this section if you don't have money you're willing to use or you haven't invested before.

TREND TRADING PSYCHOLOGY

The intensity, success, and duration of trends largely rely on two emotions: fear and greed. The greedier people are, the more trends become overvalued relative to their true (or close to their true) value. A meme coin that becomes the next hottest thing and skyrockets to a $100 million valuation is just not rational: it is based on fun, then greed, and eventually, the time at which people sell is based on fear. In this way, emotion plays a large part in trends and trend trading. Keep that in mind while viewing trends, and also keep in mind that an excess of fear or greed is liable to lead to bad decisions. Now, to keep this content original and not restate myself, I'll leave the full look at market psychology for later in the book. Feel free to skip ahead if you're interested.

TREND EXAMPLES

2020

Out of the entire dApp (shorthand for decentralized application) trend that picked up steam throughout 2020, DeFi was arguably the sub-trend that performed the best. Some popular companies within the DeFi space in 2020 were Maker (MKR), ChainLink (LINK), and Aave (AAVE). Since 2020 (in the past 15 months, as of this writing), these coins are up 17x, 950x, and 25x, respectively. Aave is the newest of the coins, hence the incredible near-1000x (95,000%) return, while the other two were established coins that took off from 2020 to 2021. The DeFi space is still growing incredibly fast.

2021

Gaming coins are a rapidly growing sector within the crypto market as projects develop new ways in which decentralized, crypto, and NFTs can be combined with gaming. A few of the popular gaming coins are Enjin Coin (ENJ), Chain Games (CHAIN), and Decentraland (MANA). Respectively, in just the first three months of 2021, these coins went up 20x, 22x, and 15x. This includes a 10x (1000%) pump from CHAIN in just *7 days*. While these coins certainly represent the best of the crypto gaming space, all could be identified through the lens of a gaming trend and then upon further research methods found within the basic analysis section below. Gaming coins still have plenty of room to grow.

TREND SCALE

The scale of trends is important to note. Generally, the larger the trend, the lower the per-asset gains. For example, a massive trend into Aave (AAVE) can cause the 95x gain experienced in 2020, while a trend into the entire DeFi space can cause the entire space to rise 3x, 5x, or 10x and a trend into the overall market might increase the total market cap by 50%, 100%, or 200%. In this way, the scale of a trend can determine the results because the percent gain is the result of the pre-trend market cap compared to the influx of money. In the case of a coin with a 10 million market cap, a trend might provide an influx of $400 million, resulting in a 40x increase. However, within the $40 billion DeFi space,[viii] $400 million would just be a 1% increase and within the $2+ trillion crypto market, $400 million is just a 0.002% drop in the bucket. Trend scale also impacts risk and volatility.

SOURCING TRENDS

Trends often start in social and sentiment-based settings, and that's the space I want to emphasize in relation to sourcing trends. Such an activity is really just predicting social momentum, and social momentum usually starts on social platforms. Social platforms, in turn, often spread information in large part through sentiment (emotion) as opposed to a purely logical approach. The fundamental value behind trends does usually exist, but it often gets blown out of proportion by sentiment. In recent years, the zenith of this has been subreddit WallStreetBets (especially in the still-developing events of GameStop and AMC short squeezes) and Elon Musk's tweets in the crypto space. In both cases, trends originated online, were based upon some degree of fundamental value, and were then blown out of proportion by social momentum. So, the question of sourcing trends is the question of identifying social momentum before it happens. This, unfortunately, is the tricky part. In my experience, insight most often comes by keeping your ear to the ground across crypto communities and influencers on multiple platforms (mainly YouTube, Twitter, Reddit, Discord, Instagram, and TikTok). You don't need to predict trends before they happen, just as they're happening, and before the peak popularity. This is the safest (not that such a strategy is safe) way of getting intro trends; not by trying to predict them, but by hitching a ride. Returns aren't the same (relative to being extremely early to a trend), but risk is equally lessened. This concludes a look into hype analysis (as I define it) and the introduction to fundamental and technical analysis. We'll move on to popular analysis metrics.

BASIC CRYPTOCURRENCY ANALYSIS

Before diving into the subject matter of this book, it is best to cover alternate forms of basic analysis for the large percentage of readers new to the whole cryptocurrency trading. In order to let advanced readers selectively choose what or what not to read, I'll insert an overview of the section below.

- Teams
- Whitepapers
- Events
- Competition
- The Big-Brother Technique
- Utility
- Sentiment Analysis
- Market Cap
- Activity
- Volatility
- Supply Mechanisms

TEAMS

Every coin or token has a team behind it that aims to provide a service, solve a problem, or in some other way provide utility and value. It is often worth your time to do some due diligence on the team behind your investments if you're looking to invest and hold for the long term. This applies to a much lesser degree if a trade is meant to be executed in a short period. However, even then, it is worth it more often than not to dig into the behind-the-scenes since doing so allows for a greater understanding of an overall situation and provides important context to all investment decisions. Take Storj, for example. This project aims to create decentralized cloud storage. The team consists of nearly 80 reputable experts from varying backgrounds, and the CEO, Ben Golub, is a professor at

Northwestern University and once taught at Harvard. In the past 30 days, as of this writing, STORJ has pumped from $0.63 to $3.27, a 400% gain. Additionally, major companies such as Google have put money in the team and the project. While none of this guarantees success, a solid foundation does massively increase the chances of long-term innovation and success. Some cryptos aren't run by a stand-alone group of developers, but rather by organizations. Cardano, an example of such, is run by three companies: IOHK, Emergo, and the Cardano Foundation, which, in turn, are managed by reputable industry leaders. ADA is up by nearly 4,000% in the past year as of this writing.

Projects with people and organizations like ADA and STORJ, as well as many others, are the real gold mines of the crypto space. The projects that survive in the long run and continue to build utility and create value are the projects that are likely to deliver massive and sustained growth. To research the team behind a project you're interested in, just do some Google searches and check out the project's website. Make sure to consult information from multiple and unbiased sources.

WHITE PAPERS

A white paper is an informational report issued by an organization about a given product, service, or general idea. White papers explain (really, sell) the concept and provide an idea and timetable of future events. Generally, this help readers understand a problem, *(tradingview.com)* Figure out how the creators of the paper aim to solve that problem, and finally form an opinion about that project.. Three types of white papers frequent the business space: the "backgrounder," which explains the background behind a product, service, or idea and provides technical, education-focused information that sells the reader. A second type of white paper is a "numbered list" that displays content in digestible, number-oriented format. For example, "10 use cases for coin CM" or "10 reasons token HL will dominate the market." A final type is a problem/solution white paper, which defines the problem that the product, service, or idea aims to solve. All three types of common and should be noted while looking into the white paper of your favorite crypto project to understand context. White papers are used within the crypto space to explain novel concepts (or perhaps not-novel concepts) and the technicalities, vision, and plans surrounding a given project. All professional crypto projects will have a white paper, typically found on their website. A project raising money through an ICO (initial coin offering) all but requires a white paper. Reading the white paper will give you a better understanding of the project than practically any other single source of accessible information. Below are a few websites that store such crypto white papers.

- ◆ All Crypto White Papers -
  https://www.allcryptowhitepapers.com/
- ◆ Crypto Rating
  https://cryptorating.eu/whitepapers/
- ◆ CoinDesk
  https://www.coindesk.com/tag/white-papers

EVENTS

A great way to analyze the potential of a coin or token, whether in the short term, midterm, or long term, is through an understanding of upcoming events. A few popular crypto event calendars are below.

- CoinMarketCal - https://coinmarketcal.com/en/
- CoinEvents - https://www.coinevents.co/
- CoinCalendar - https://coinscalendar.com/

With these websites, all upcoming launches, partnerships, airdrops, forks/swaps, or any other notable event can be viewed for most cryptocurrencies. The simple number of upcoming coin events, not to mention the quality, can tell you a lot about a project. Then, reading into each event can provide a step forward in terms of really understanding how a project will evolve over time. Often, coins will pump 10%, 20%, or beyond on the day of an event. However, keep in mind that crypto is not a fully efficient market (remember the EMH), so while events upcoming in the extreme short-term are often priced into the value of the coin or token, the same may not be said about events a few weeks or months out. Therefore, if you do buy based on events, it is a much better bet to do so on upcoming events happening at least a few weeks out of the current date. Even then, risk is involved because if enough traders buy early enough, with the intent of dumping the day of an event after an assumed pump, the price can instead crash even if the event is good news. So, weigh all of these event-related factors while considering how or whether to invest in a coin or token and, regardless, make sure to keep informed on events happening across the market and within the realm of the assets you hold.

COMPETITION

As within all aspects of business, competition is a must for understanding a company's relative situation in a given market. Within the highly volatile crypto market, this applies to an even greater degree. However, within niches of the crypto market, such as web 3.0, decentralized storage, etc., there's plenty of space for multiple companies. This falls back to the Big-Brother concept, which dictates that projects offering a small twist off of another larger project, can perform exceedingly well, despite established competition.

THE BIG-BROTHER TECHNIQUE

The Big-Brother technique, a creation of the popular crypto influencer *Ivan On Tech* (links to his channel are available in the resource section), is an important and extremely easy concept within the sphere of competition and dictates how and why some cryptos can blow up. The technique relies on trends; within such trends (such as DeFi, FinTech, gaming coins), projects that often go parabolic are the ones that have a similar, brother-like project and differ through some positive alteration. This works because investors aren't as likely to embrace a new technology or idea as a new project that differs from an already popular coin in only small ways. For example, Ethereum, (ETH), when it first came out was just like Bitcoin (BTC), except ETH utilized smart contracts. Then, Cardano was like Ethereum, except Cardano utilized a modified proof-of-stake algorithm to make its network more scalable. Recently, the exchange Uniswap (UNI) served as the big brother to the exchange PancakeSwap (CAKE), which offers much lower fees. In all these cases, traders were familiar with the general concepts and ideas behind the projects and the new projects that were generally the same but had a few key alterations.

UTILITY

Utility within a coin or token is one of the most important aspects of due diligence since understanding the current and long-term utility and value behind a coin or token allows for a much clearer analysis of potential. Utility is defined as being useful and functional. Crypto coins or tokens with utility have real, practical uses: they don't just exist but rather serve to solve a problem or offer a service. Coins with the most functional current uses and use cases are likely to succeed as opposed to those without continued purpose, use, and innovation. Here are a few case studies:

- Bitcoin (BTC) serves as a reliable and long-term store of value, akin to "digital gold."
- Ether (ETH) allows dApp and Smart Contracts to be created on top of the Ethereum blockchain.

- Storj (STORJ) can be used to store data in the cloud in a decentralized manner, similar to Google Drive and Dropbox.

- IOTA (IOTA) offers completely free transactions to be used for small, daily payments.

- Basic Attention Token (BAT) is used within the Brave browser to earn rewards and send tips to creators.

- Golem (GNT) is a kind of global supercomputer that offers rentable computing resources in exchange for GNT tokens.

All of these coins or tokens have real, practical utility. Projects that have utility and work on constantly improving utility (much of this hinges on the team, as previously covered) will have greater success in the long term.

SENTIMENT ANALYSIS

Sentiment analysis is the smart way of saying "figuring out what people think." Understanding sentiment towards a person, brand, coin, token, trend, etc., is very useful information, because, as mentioned, social momentum often predicts trends. Today, software can analyze social media websites and the wider internet for sentiment (for example, searching for the amount of positive versus negative words in tweets mentioning "Bitcoin" in the past 24 hours) and provide this information in an easy-to-understand manner. This is the easiest way to use sentiment; you can also do your own research by combing through websites or simply reading the titles of new articles. Sentiment analysis is frequently used in the business world and is something to add to your crypto-analysis toolbox. Below are several tools (all of which are free) that can be used to understand the sentiment of the entire market, the entire investment community, or individual assets (most reflect individual assets).

Crypto Fear & Greed Index - https://alternative.me/crypto/fear-and-greed-index/

This index shows whether crypto investors are generally feeling bold or scared. The lower the number (between 0 and 100), the more fear, and the higher the number, the greater the greediness.

Bulls & Bears Index - https://www.augmento.ai/Bitcoin-sentiment/

The bulls & bears index analyzes social media in relation to bullish/bearish sentiment about Bitcoin (BTC). The data is collected from Twitter, Reddit, and Bitcointalk. An alternative Bitcoin sentiment index can be found at https://www.bittsanalytics.com/sentiment-index/BTC.

Santiment - https://app.santiment.net/

Santiment is a free service (paid options are available, please note that the Santiment paid plans are not for the sentiment tools, which are free) that offers cryptocurrency sentiment tools, which, quote, allows users to "find data-driven investing opportunities." Santrends identifies the top 10 emerging trends, and Santiment insights https://insights.santiment.net/ provides various insights into crypto sentiment and the overall market.

MARKET CAP

Market cap, shorthand for market capitalization, is the total market value of a cryptocurrency. Shares (as in the stock market) are represented by coins or tokens in the cryptocurrency markets. Market cap is a very widely used metric that basically identifies the size of a project. For example, using market cap, we know that Bitcoin is worth (currently) $1.1 trillion, while OVR (OVR) is $177 million. In this way, through market cap, we can estimate volatility, potential upside, and a host of other factors that influence investment decisions (just as an interesting tidbit, I list "potential upside" because of the following idea: let's assume that 1 billion will be invested in a project. If $1 billion was put into Bitcoin, with a market cap of $1.1 trillion, the price movement would be practically nothing. However, if $1 billion is put into OVR, the price and market cap will near 10x. To 10x Bitcoin, $11 trillion would be necessary, an absolutely insane number. In this way, market cap can determine potential upside, as well as volatility).

To find the market cap of a coin or token, just multiply the price by the total number of coins or tokens. This is the equation: market cap = cost per unit x number of units. For example, a coin with a circulating supply (circulating supply and other supply mechanisms will be covered shortly) of 1,000,000 and a price of $10 per coin has a market cap of $10 million because 1,000,000 x 10 = 10,000,000. Here are some other market cap equations, which will conclude our market cap section:

- Helium (HNT)

$18 (price) x 77,995,503 (supply) = $1,403,919,054 (market cap)

- Binance Coin (BNB)

$475 x 154,532,785 = $73,403,072,875

- PancakeSwap (CAKE)

$22 x 151,000,000 =

You enter this one (or calculate an estimate in your head)!

ACTIVITY

Correctly judging activity metrics enables an understanding of utility within a coin, characteristics of a coin, size, probable trends, and more. We'll cover three of such metrics, all of which are easily discoverable and simple. First up: volume.

VOLUME

Trading volume, known just as "volume," is the number of coins or tokens traded within a specified time frame. Volume can show the relative health of a certain coin or the overall market. For example, as of this writing, Bitcoin (BTC) has a 24h volume of $46 billion, while Litecoin (LTC), within the same timeframe, traded $7 billion. A useful statistic within volume is the ratio between the market cap and volume. For example, continuing with the two coins above, Bitcoin has a market cap of $1.1 trillion and a volume of $46 billion, meaning that $1 in every $24 on the network was traded in the past 24 hours. Litecoin has a market cap of $16.7 billion and a 24h volume of $7 billion, meaning that $1 of every $2.3 on the network was traded in the past 24 hours (it gets crazier than this as of this writing Tether (USDT) has a market cap of $44 billion and 24h volume of $114 billion). Through an understanding of volume, other information about a coin, such as popularity, volatility, utility, and so on, can be better understood. In this way, understanding volume and volume trends can be helpful in basic analysis and understanding your trades. Below are a few sites that provide easy and free information about volume:

- ◆ CoinMarketCap - coinmarketcap.com
- ◆ CoinGecko – coingecko.com
- ◆ Yahoo Finance Crypto – finance.yahoo.com

ACTIVE ADDRESSES

Active addresses are the number of unique addresses (addresses can be thought of as leading to bank accounts, within which crypto is stored) that participate in one or more successful transactions within a given timeframe and within given parameters defining "active." Basically, it can be thought of as the number of people trading within a crypto ecosphere. Understanding relative activity (relative to historical data) can be a useful part of understanding the overall market trends of a given asset, as well as in predicting price. When researching active addresses (specifically within the linked site below, but also through most other related sites), you can choose the parameters of activity, such as activity in addresses with a balance of over \$1 million, addresses with profit or loss, and various others. Check out Bitcoin's active addresses below:

♦ Glassnode Studio

studio.glassnode.com/metrics?a=BTC&m=addresses.ActiveCount

AVERAGE HOLDING TIME

The average holding time is the average time an investor holds a cryptocurrency. The AHT is useful because it allows for an understanding of how the crypto is traded, for example, whether it is a short-term flip or a mid-term hold. Given the overall newness of the crypto market, the entire industry is very volatile, and the AHT, relative to other securities markets, is quite low. That said, what matters more is the difference within the market. As of this writing, the typical hold time of Bitcoin on Coinbase is 63 days. While, relative to stocks, that number is low, it is on the higher side within the crypto space; to compare, the average holding times of Storj (STORJ) and Enjin Coin (ENJ) are, respectively, 8 days and 1 day. Note that the ATH metric is constrained within large central exchanges, such as Coinbase, since the data cannot be collected from all crypto users but rather from a centralized company that manages its users' money. I especially recommend Coinbase for this, and while the overall ATH metric isn't a major part of analysis, it certainly is a nice and easy tool to consider. This concludes our trifecta of activity metrics.

VOLATILITY

I've chosen not to lump volatility in with the activity metrics despite volatility, to some extent, fitting into that box. I've done this because volatility is much more important as a subject to the wider world of investments, as well as specifically to the crypto market. Volatility is why many people don't get into the crypto market; it is also why many do since it allows for the monstrous gains that many traders are experiencing.

Volatility is basically a measure of deviation: how fast, how often, and how much prices vary (simply put, the "size of change"). Since volatility is highly correlated with risk, it can be thought of as a risk metric. Volatility is typically calculated through standard deviation and variance. Histogram charts are a simple method by which to judge volatility (measured in delta, gamma, vega, and theta).

Different asset classes are known for certain levels of volatility, and this, more often than not, is why or why not an investor gets into a certain market. Here is a simple look at several different asset classes:[4]

- ♦ Cash
- ♦ Bonds
- ♦ Real Estate
- ♦ Stocks
- ♦ Cryptocurrencies

Given the above list, I'll rearrange these asset classes according to volatility (least to most).

- ♦ Cash
- ♦ Bonds
- ♦ Real Estate
- ♦ Stocks
- ♦ Cryptocurrencies

---

[4] This is a simplified and stylized view of asset classes. It is not a complete list.

So, cash has a very low measure of volatility and people who hold a large percentage of their money in cash are generally risk-averse. Real estate is more volatile than cash, so people who get into such a space must be a little more comfortable with risk. The stock market (especially certain areas of the market, such as penny stocks and options) carries higher risk levels compared to real estate. Then, at the high end of the spectrum, cryptocurrency holds the spot as, quite arguably, the most volatile type of asset on the list. We've already established that people often choose a strategy in their investments through the lens of volatility; retirees are likely to choose conservative investments, such as bonds and blue chip stocks, while 20-somethings may choose assets near the upper end of the list, such as smaller-cap stocks and cryptocurrencies.

Understanding the relative placement in terms of volatility of your chosen investments is essential to determining a long-term strategy and making rational decisions while choosing how to invest, specifically through technical analysis, but also in all investment decisions throughout your life. Some people are comfortable with more volatility, others with less, and either way, that's fine; just do you and do your research. Also, hodl![5]

SUPPLY MECHANISMS

Supply mechanisms are the processes by which supply takes place. Supply, in terms of crypto, relates to the number of coins or tokens that exist and will exist, as well as how these coins can be added or taken away from circulation. Supply mechanisms are important because supply and demand form the backstory to all economic activity. Supply affects demand and alters how cryptocurrencies are fueled, operate, and grow. We will briefly cover the concepts of maximum and circulating supply (two of the central and most widely used supply-related

---

[5] HODL is a common term used in crypto that's a variation of the word "hold" and means the same. I mean to point out that in volatile markets, it's often better to hold in the long term than to make an emotional and irrational decision either to sell or buy.

metrics). Afterward, we will look at several different types of supply mechanisms to arrive at a full understanding of the supply mechanics behind cryptos and how all this may affect investment decisions.

MAXIMUM SUPPLY

The maximum supply is the max number of coins that can ever exist for a cryptocurrency. The maximum supply (or the lack of such) is pre-set, such as Bitcoin's 21-million-coin limit. Some coins, like Bitcoin, add more coins into the network over time until the maximum supply is reached, while others begin at their maximum supply and others still have no maximum supply. Once a maximum supply is hit, no more coins will ever be procured and, for coins such as Bitcoin, that limit will eventually be reached through an "issuance rate" which defines the influx of new coins and typically decreases over time. Contrary to this process, some coins, including Ether (ETH), have a set issuance rate and no maximum supply. To fully understand a cryptocurrency, you may want to check out its maximum supply, as well as the circulating supply (below), and this can be done through popular crypto websites such as coinmarketcap.com, coingecko.com, and others. More information about the supply mechanisms of a given cryptocurrency can usually be found on the project website.

CIRCULATING SUPPLY

The circulating supply is the total number of publicly available coins or tokens. In some cases, such as that of Bitcoin, the circulating supply will increase until the maximum supply of 21 million coins is reached. In other cases, the number of circulating coins goes down, often through the process of burning, and thus the intrinsic value of the asset should increase since less and less will be available. So, the circulating supply displays the current number of tradable coins, and the number of tradable coins can either increase or decrease with time.

FIXED SUPPLY - DEFLATIONARY ASSETS

Fixed-supply cryptocurrencies have an algorithmic limit to coin supply. Bitcoin, as mentioned, is a fixed-supply asset since no more coins can possibly be created once 21 million have been put into circulation. Currently, nearly 90% of Bitcoins have been mined, and around 0.5% of the total supply is being lost per year. As a result of halving (covered below), Bitcoin will hit its maximum supply around 2140. Many other cryptocurrencies (sourced from the website cryptoli.st—check them out for yourself if you're interested in other crypto lists) such as Binance Coin (BNB), Cardano (ADA), Litecoin (LTC), and ChainLink (LINK) operate with a fixed-supply. Given the popularity of the mentioned coins, the fixed-supply model obviously must hold some benefits; the most apparent of which being that such systems are deflationary. Deflationary assets are assets in which the total supply decreases over time, and therefore each unit increases in value. For example, say you're stranded on a desert island with 10 other people, and each person has 1 bottle of water. Since some people may presumably drink their water, the total supply of 100 bottles of water can only decrease. This makes the water a deflationary asset. As the total supply shrinks, each water bottle becomes worth increasingly more. Say, now, there are only 20 water bottles left. Each of the 20 water bottles is worth as much as 5 water bottles were once worth when all 100 were being circulated. In this way, long-term holders of deflationary assets experience an increase in value of their holdings because the fundamental value relative to the whole (in the water-bottle example, 1 bottle out of 100 is 1%, while 1 out of 20 is 5%, making each bottle worth 5x more) has increased. Overall, a fixed-supply and deflationary model, much like digital gold, will increase the fundamental value of each coin or token over time and create value through scarcity.

What happens when all the coins are in circulation?

When the max limit is reached, and all coins have been mined, the reward system (specifically of Bitcoin and likely of other coins as well) must change since miners can no longer directly earn crypto through validating transactions and adding blocks to a blockchain. The solution to this problem is simply to switch over to a fee-based system in which users directly pay fees to miners alongside each transaction. Given the competitive marketplace, the fees should stay low, and the situation should continue as the win-win that it is.

UNLIMITED SUPPLY – INFLATIONARY ASSETS

Remember, each unit of a deflationary asset increases in value relative to the total supply over time because the total supply goes down. With inflationary assets, new money enters the total circulating supply and causes all the other money to lose value. Let's return to the island scenario in which 10 people have 10 water bottles. Assume that our stranded island-goers are discovered, and a plane will fly over the island and deliver 20 bottles of water every day until the group can be rescued. Each person will now receive 2 water bottles per day, equivalent to 20% of their total supply. As you can imagine, each water bottle is now worth much less because each person in need of water will get more every day. In 30 days, the total supply (ignoring drunk water) will be at 700 bottles, which means each bottle accounts for 0.14% of the total supply instead of the 1% each bottle was once worth. This is a 7x decrease in value and reflects the effects of sustained inflation. The same principle can transfer over into securities and cryptocurrencies; many coins have an unlimited supply and experience inflation as a result. Popular coins using an unlimited supply model are Ethereum (ETH), Dogecoin (DOGE), and numerous others. However, is an unlimited supply a bad thing?

Let's consider Ethereum (ETH), which has an unlimited supply. Eighteen million ETHs are mined per year, which is a set number that doesn't and won't change. So, given an infinite amount of time, an infinite number of coins could be produced because the coins can keep being made out of nowhere, just like how governments print money. However, while this may sound like a problem because of inflation, inflation over time will actually decrease given that the total supply is growing, but the additions per year stay the same. Example: If 250 million Ether coins exist, inflation must be at 7.2%, since 18/250 is 0.072. However, in 10 years, when 180 new coins have been minted, and the total supply is at 430 million, the same number of coins (18 million) are produced, and inflation is down to 4%. Another ten years down the road and inflation is at 2.9%, and twenty years after that, it is down to 1.8%. In this way, inflation decreases over time. So, while inflation still certainly exists for coins with unlimited supplies, the rate of inflation becomes less and less of a problem over time. Also, inflation is thought of as being good for the economy because it forces people to spend or otherwise use their money for that money not to lose value. All that said, while most cryptocurrencies have a limited supply and most investors like the idea of deflationary assets, neither limited nor unlimited models are completely better than the alternative. As always, you should do your research and understand what you're getting into, and while supply mechanisms should certainly factor into your decision, they should not be the deciding factor (in most cases).

BURNING

The term "burned" refers to coins being permanently removed from circulation; burning is a supply mechanism that enables coins to be taken out of circulation, hence acting as a deflationary tool and increasing the value of each other coin in the network (this concept, if you're familiar, is much like company buy backs in the stock market). Burns are usually performed by the team and project behind a cryptocurrency to drive the price upward through deflation. Burning can be done in several different ways: one of these ways is by simply sending the coins to an inaccessible wallet, which is called an "eater address." In this case, while the tokens haven't technically been removed from the total supply, the circulating supply has effectively gone down. Currently, around 3 million Bitcoins (200+ billion of value) have been lost through this process. Tokens can also be burned by coding a burn function into the protocols that govern a token, but the far more popular option is through the mentioned eater addresses. As with halving, (immediately below) scarcity creates value, and burning increases scarcity and, as a result, value.

HALVING

Halving is a supply mechanism that governs the rate at which coins are added to a fixed-supply cryptocurrency. The idea and process were popularized by Bitcoin, which halves every 4 years. Halving is set in motion by a programmed reduction in mining rewards; block rewards are the rewards given to the miners (really, the computers) that process and validate transactions in a given blockchain network. From 2016 to 2020, all the computers (called the nodes) in the Bitcoin network collectively earned 12.5 Bitcoin every 10 minutes, and that was the number of Bitcoins entering circulation. However, following May 11th, 2020, the rewards dropped to 6.25 Bitcoin per the same timeframe. In this way, for every 210,000 blocks mined, which equates to roughly every four years, the block rewards will continue to halve until the max limit of 21 million coins is reached around the year 2040. Thus, halving is likely to increase the value of Bitcoin and other cryptocurrencies by decreasing supply while not altering demand. Scarcity, as mentioned, drives value, and limited supply combined with growing demand creates greater and greater scarcity. For this reason, halving has historically driven the price of Bitcoin up and will likely be a long-term growth catalyst. This concludes basic cryptocurrency analysis and the entirety of part 1.

PART 2: TECHNICAL ANALYSIS

A look into all aspects of technical analysis.

TECHNICAL ANALYSIS

Part 1 covers all bases of crypto analysis, and this section develops the subject matter of this book: a guide and reference tool for those interested in crypto technical analysis. Below is a brief outline of part 2; please consult the table of contents or the index for further information:

STARTING OUT WITH TECHNICAL ANALYSIS

As you read the rest of this book, I suggest you consult the resource section (check the table of contents for page numbers) to access a range of cryptocurrency resources. Resources include top podcasts, YouTube channels, other books, and more, all of which enable you to stay up-to-date with the crypto market and pursue alternate learning methods.

STRATEGY

At the end of this section, we'll revisit the concept of a cumulative strategy. For now, be on the lookout for connections between individual tools and indicators, and think about building a trading "toolbox" that includes a multitude of tools, all of which build upon one another and allow for efficient, streamlined, and profitable picks.

TYPES OF CHARTS

Charts are the foundation of technical analysis; they form the basis by which prices can be examined and patterns can be found. Charts, on one level, are simple, and on another, deep and complex. We'll begin with the basics; different types of charts and their different uses. '

LINE CHART

A line chart is a chart that represents prices through one single line. Most charts are line charts because, although they contain less information than popular alternatives, they are extremely easy to understand. Robinhood and Coinbase (both of which target their services towards less experienced investors) have line charts as the default chart type, while institutions aimed towards a more experienced audience, such as Charles Schwab and Binance, use other chat forms.

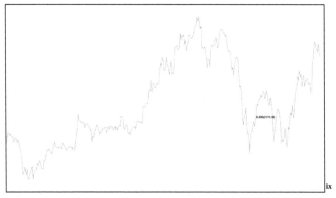

(tradingview.com) Figure 10: Line Chart[x]

CANDLESTICK CHART

Candlestick charts are a much more useful form of displaying information about a coin and are the chart of choice for most investors. Within a given period, candlestick charts have a wide "real body" and may be red or green (another common color scheme is empty and filled real bodies) If it is red (filled in), the close was lower than the open (meaning it went down). If the real body is red (empty), the close was higher than the open (meaning it went up). Above and below the real bodies are the "wicks" also known as "shadows." Wicks show the high and low prices of the period's trading. So, combining what we know, if the upper wick (aka the upper shadow) is close to the real body, the high the coin or token reached during the day is near the closing price. Hence, the opposite also applies. You will need to have a solid understanding of candlestick charts, so I suggest you visit a site such as tradingview.com to get comfortable.

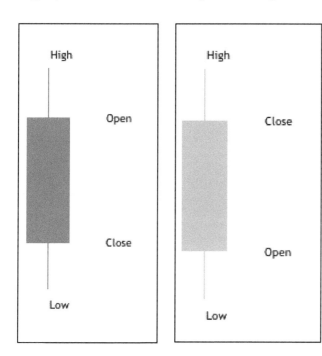

(tradingview.com) Figure 11: Bearish Candle[xi]

(tradingview.com) Figure 12: Bullish Candle[xii]

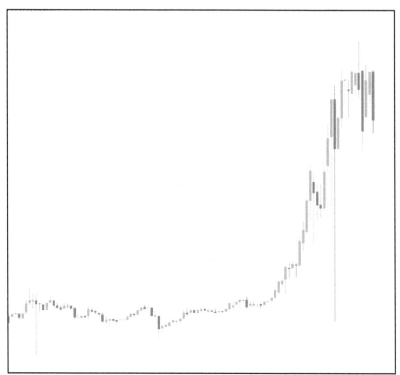

(tradingview.com) Figure 13: Candlestick Chart[xiii]

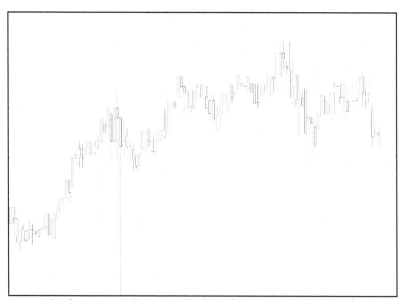

(tradingview.com) Figure 14: Candlestick Chart - Expanded View[xiv]

RENKO CHART

Renko charts only show price movement and ignore time and volume. Renko comes from the Japanese term "renga," meaning "bricks." Renko charts use bricks (also known as boxes), typically red/green or white/black. Renko boxes only form at the top or bottom right corner of the proceeding box, and the next box can only form if the price passes the top or bottom of the previous box. For example, if the predefined amount is "$1" (think of this as similar to time intervals on candlestick charts), then the next box can only form once it passes either $1 above or $1 below the price of the previous box. These charts simplify and "smooth out" trends into easy-to-understand patterns while removing random price action. This can make conducting technical analysis easier since patterns such as support and resistance levels are much more blatantly displayed.

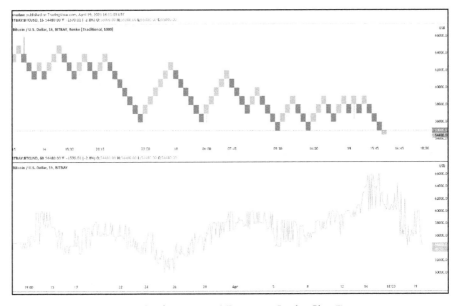

A: *(tradingview.com)* Figure 15: Renko Chart[xv]

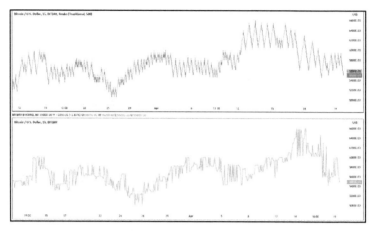

B: *(tradingview.com)* Figure 16: Renko Chart #2[xvi]

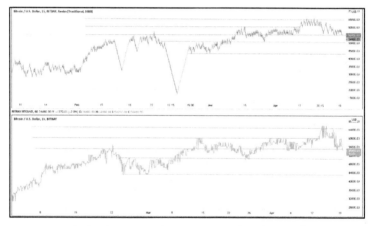

C: *(tradingview.com)* Figure 17: Renko Chart #3[xvii]

A: Close-up of a Renko chart. Notice the boxes and the simplified patterns.

B: Renko chart compared to a line chart.

C: Plotted support and resistance lines on a Renko chart.

POINT & FIGURE CHART

While point and *(tradingview.com)* Figure (P&F) charts aren't as well-known as the others on this list, they do have a long history and a reputation as one of the simplest charts used to identify good entry and exit points. Like Renko charts, P&F charts don't directly account for the passage of time. Rather, Xs and Os are stacked in columns; each letter represents a chosen price movement (just like the blocks in Renko charts). Xs represent a rising price, and Os represent a falling price. Look at this sequence:

```
    X
X O X
X O
X
```

Let's say the chosen price movement is $10. We must start at the bottom left: the 3 Xs indicate that the price rose $30, the 2 Os signify a $20 drop, and then the final 2 Xs represent a $20 rise. Time is irrelevant.

xviii

(tradingview.com) Figure 18: Point & Figure Chart[xix]

HEIKIN-ASHI

Heikin-Ashi (hik-in-aw-she) charts are a simpler, smoothed version of candlestick charts. They function almost the same way as candlestick charts, (candles, wicks, shadows, etc.), except HA charts smooth price data over two periods instead of one. This, essentially, makes Heikin-Ashi preferable to many traders versus candlestick charts because patterns and trends can be more easily spotted and false signals (small, meaningless moves) are, in large part, omitted. That said, the simpler appearance does obscure some data relative to candlesticks, which is partly why Heikin-Ashis haven't yet replaced candlesticks. So, I suggest that you experiment with both chart types and *(tradingview.com)* Figure out what best fits your style and ability to discern trends.

A: *(tradingview.com)* Figure 19: Heikin-Ashi Chart[xx]

B: *(tradingview.com)* Figure 20: Heikin-Ashi Chart #2[xxi]

A: Note that the trends on the Heikin-Ashi chart are smoother and more discernible than on the lower candlestick chart.

B: Note that significant upward trends have continuously green candles without the lower shadow, while strong downward trends have continuous red candles without the upper shadow.

CHARTING RESOURCES

♦ TradingView

   tradingview.com (best overall, best social)

♦ CoinMarketCap

   coinmarketcap.com (simple, easy)

♦ CryptoWatch

   cryptowat.ch (very established, best for bots)

♦ CryptoView

   cryptoview.com (very customizable)

♦ GoCharting

   gocharting.com (good free options)

♦ Coinigy

   coinigy.com (great range of pairs and exchanges)

♦ Coin 360

   coin360.com (unique UI, check this one out!)

♦ Altrady

   altrady.com (scanners, handy tools)

♦ CoinCheckup

   coincheckup.com (simple)

CHART PATTERN CLASSIFICATIONS

Chart patterns are classified in order to quickly understand role and purpose. I'll take a brief moment to run through a few of these classifications.

BULLISH

All bullish patterns are likely to result in the outcome being favorable to the upside, so, for example, a bullish pattern may result in a 10% uptrend.

BEARISH

All bearish patterns are likely to result in the outcome being favorable to the downside, so, for example, a bearish pattern may result in a 10% downtrend.

CANDLESTICK

Candlestick patterns apply specifically to candlestick charts, not to all charts. This is because candlestick patterns rely on information that can only come across in a candle (body and wick) format.

NUMBER OF BARS/CANDLES

The number of bars or candles in a pattern is usually no more than three.

CONTINUATION

Continuation patterns signal that the pre-pattern trend is more likely than not to continue. So, for example, if continuation pattern X forms at the top of an uptrend, then the uptrend is likely to continue.

BREAKOUT

A breakout is a move above resistance or below support. Breakout patterns indicate that such a move is probable. The direction of that breakout is specific to the pattern.

REVERSAL

A reversal is a change in the direction of price. A reversal pattern indicates that the direction of the price is likely to change (so, an uptrend would become a downtrend, and a downtrend would become an uptrend).

RISK MANAGEMENT

Along with classifications, I'd like to take a moment to cover trading strategies and methods that alter the amount risk exposure.

STOP LOSS

A stop loss is an extremely useful tool that enables sell orders to be placed and executed once a price reaches a certain level. This enables risk management through control over the maximum possible loss (excluding slippage). We will consider this situation: You're placing a risky bet on a breakout over $40. If the price breaks out, the next series resistance level is at $46, representing a 15% gain. In this case, you may want to place a stop-loss order at $37. If the price ever reaches $37, your entire position will be immediately sold. Essentially, this means that the downside risk is limited to 7.5% while the there's a good chance of the upside being 15%. You can alter the stop loss to cap your potential risk at whatever you want, whether it be 5%, 15%, or 30%. Make sure to account for volatility to prevent false signals from triggering stop losses.

TRAILING STOP LOSS

Trailing stop losses are an advanced form of stop losses that move with the price. For example, given the example directly above, instead of placing a stop loss at $37, you could place a stop loss at $3 below the market price. This way, the order will still execute at $37, but if the price moves to $43, the order will then execute at $40. Hence, risk is limited no matter the price. Trailing stop losses can be set as fixed-dollar amounts, or as percentages. You must also choose the degree to which the order will trail the price (meaning, should the stop loss execute if the price is $3 below the previous day's close, the previous hour's close, and so on.

LONG VERSUS SHORT TRADING

The terms "long trade" and "short trade" will be used throughout this section. "Long" and "buy" are used interchangeably; for example, you may establish a long position, which means you bought coins, or you may be "long on Bitcoin," which means you bought and hold Bitcoins. "Short" refers to shorting an asset, which is betting that a price will go down. Shorting is riskier and much less popular than buying and owning shares. Many of the popular centralized exchanges in the US and around the world don't allow shorting, and therefore only buying long applies to you. However, for full clarity and for those using exchanges around the world that do accept shorting (shorting services will likely become more common as the industry grows), I have included shorting in the descriptions of chart patterns, oscillators, indicators, and throughout the rest of this book.

CHART PATTERNS

Before moving on to candlestick-specific formations, about a dozen basic chart patterns should be looked at. These are general shapes formed within charts (whether line, candlestick, or others) that can affect and predict future price action. All are usually discernable on a wider timeframe, as opposed to the short-term timespan of most candlestick formations. The most important and common of these patterns are included in the Essentials section at the end of this chapter. That said, don't underestimate any, and I suggest you read carefully into each.

- Triangles
    - Symmetrical
    - Ascending
    - Descending
- Price Channel
- Rounding Bottom
- Cup and Handle
- Pennant
- Flag
- Rectangles
- Wedge
- Head and Shoulders
- Double Bottom/Double Top
- Triple Bottom/Triple Top
- Bump and Run

TRIANGLES

Triangle patterns are the most well-known formation; they're practically synonymous with popular knowledge of technical analysis. Three sub-categories of triangle formations exist, all of which are continuation patterns (signaling that a trend with continue in the form of a breakout) Ideally, any of the triangle formations described below could tell you if an uptrend will keep trending upward or if a downtrend will continue down. Triangle patterns are relatively common across crypto charts and, if traded upon correctly, should serve as reliable indicators. Below is a look into each triangle pattern, along with real examples.

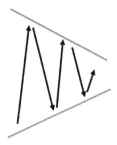  

Symmetrical Triangle   Ascending Triangle   Descending Triangle

6

---

[6] Photo credit: 1investing.in

ASCENDING TRIANGLE

Ascending triangles are continuation patterns that form a horizontal upper trendline and a diagonally rising lower trendline. Typically, a bullish breakout will occur near the tip of the triangle (really, it will occur once the trading range diminishes enough for buyer support to recover and push through resistance, which is normally close to the tip). The upper trendline (the resistance) then becomes the new support line. Thus, a simple ascending triangle short-term trade involves buying a long order once two bars close above the breakout line (to omit false signals) and setting a stop-loss order at or just under the breakout line.

(tradingview.com) Figure 21: Ascending Triangle[xxii]

(tradingview.com) Figure 22: Ascending Triangle #2[xxiii]

DESCENDING TRIANGLE

Descending triangles are the opposite of ascending triangles: They consist of a horizontal lower trendline and a diagonally sinking upper trendline (meaning the low stays low, and the high gets lower). The descending triangle is a bearish continuation pattern, meaning that a price is more likely to downtrend as the trading range decreases. A simple trade involving a descending triangle involves shorting once two bars close under the lower trendline and setting a stop-loss order at or just above the breakout line.

(tradingview.com) Figure 23: Descending Triangle[xxiv]

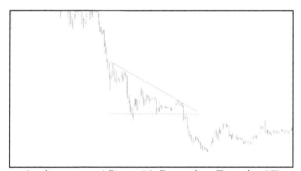

(tradingview.com) Figure 24: Descending Triangle #2[xxv]

SYMMETRICAL TRIANGLE

While both ascending and descending triangles have a direction (up or down) and indicate a directional movement (also up or down), symmetrical triangles have neither. Symmetrical triangles represent near-equal bullish and bearish power and trade within a declining price range (basically, lower highs and higher lows). Eventually, the price range declines to a point (near the tip of the triangle) at which a breakout is likely to occur. The breakout can be either positive or negative. It's tougher to trade upon symmetrical triangles since the direction can't be assumed, so the best course of action is to place an order as soon as possible after the breakout occurs and confirms—a long position if the breakout is positive, or a short position if the breakout is negative. A stop-loss order can then be placed, respectively, at the upper trendline or bottom trendline of the triangle. To weed out false signals (called "head fakes" in this case), you should watch for a spike in volume and a few closes beyond the trendline before placing an order. All that said, symmetrical triangles do tend to break out in the direction of the move pre-formation. It is by no means something to assume or trade upon, rather something to keep in mind given the strategy outlined above.

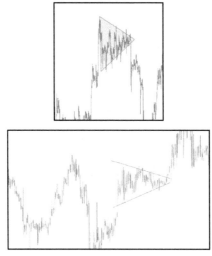

(tradingview.com) Figure 25: Symmetrical Triangle[xxvi]
(tradingview.com) Figure 26: Symmetrical Triangle #2[xxvii]

PRICE CHANNEL

A price channel (less commonly referred to as a trading channel) is a foundational formation formed by a pair of parallel trend lines advancing in any direction.[7] Often, price channels form support and resistance levels; hence, prices tend to oscillate between such lines. If trendlines are broken through, whether above or below, the result is a breakout. Many of the patterns in this chapter involve price channels in some form and attempt to predict breakouts, in part, through them.

 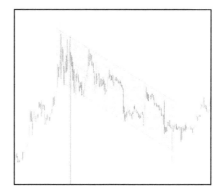

(tradingview.com) Figure 27: Price Channel[xxviii]
(tradingview.com) Figure 28: Price Channel[xxix]

---

[7] The different directions form either descending price channels, ascending price channels, or neutral (horizontal) price channels.

ROUNDING BOTTOM

Rounding bottoms are the "cup" of the candle and handle formation, as elaborated upon directly below. Rounding bottoms (also known as saucer bottoms) are found following uptrends, form the shape of a "U," and signify a long-term reversal. This pattern may take weeks or months to form. It indicates that selling pressure pushed the price down and the subsequent lower price resulted in an influx of buyers and a solid base, which led to those buyers pushing the price back up. The cup and handle is a popular variation of this pattern, which is known to be more reliable than the rounding bottom given its relative lack of false signals.

(tradingview.com) Figure 29: Rounding Bottom[xxx]

(tradingview.com) Figure 30: Rounding Bottom #2[xxxi]

CUP AND HANDLE

The cup and handle is a bullish continuation pattern defined by William O'Neil in 1988. The pattern forms a rounded U-shape and a handle that trends slightly downward. Cups with more gradual U-shaped bottoms provide better signals relative to distinct "V" bottoms. Handles form above the midpoint of the cups, and neither cups nor handles should be overly deep. In theory, the cup and handle formation indicate that price has tested a high, hence incurring selling pressure and consolidating the price back downwards before retesting the high, briefly pulling back, and then breaking resistance and moving higher. Cup and handle patterns are generally identified with a wider timespan (typically within the range of seven weeks up to sixty-five weeks) and signal longer-term price movements, which may occur over months or years. Some traders estimate the substance of the breakout by measuring the increase from the bottom of the cup to the top right of the cup and adding that percent to the end of the price channel. While that rule can serve as a general estimation, it isn't decidedly accurate. As the crypto industry settles into itself, cup and handle patterns will likely become more commonplace. Note the varying slope of the cups and the variation in the length of the handles in both photos.

(tradingview.com) Figure 31: Cup and Handle[xxxii]

(tradingview.com) Figure 32: Cup and Handle #2[xxxiii]

PENNANT

A pennant is a continuation pattern that appears after a large positive or negative jump. The pennant formation consolidates subsequent to the jump and typically continues in the same direction. Pennants only differ from symmetrical triangles through the flagpole, which is the rapid uptrend or downtrend. Apart from the flagpole, the pattern is just a symmetrical triangle and should be treated as such, except in that the breakout is extremely likely to continue in the initial direction. To trade upon pennants, simply follow the triangle rules of buying after a confirmed positive breakout or shorting following a confirmed negative breakout (and, of course, don't forget stop-losses).

(tradingview.com) Figure 33: Pennant[xxxiv]

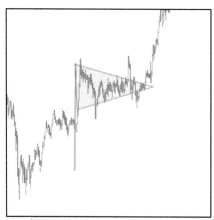

(tradingview.com) Figure 34: Pennant #2[xxxv]

FLAG

The flag pattern is very similar to the pennant pattern, except pennants form a triangle after the flagpole, while flags form two parallel lines.[8] Most of the pennant rules apply to flags; the formation represents a likely continuation of previous trends and can be traded upon accordingly.

(tradingview.com) Figure 35: Flag[xxxvi]

(tradingview.com) Figure 36: Flag #2[xxxvii]

---

[8] The proper difference would be "converging versus parallel trend lines."

RECTANGLES

Rectangle patterns help chart viewers identify support and resistance levels (they're just a horizontal price channel). This is useful in discerning other patterns and in identifying good entry/exit prices.

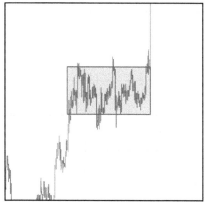 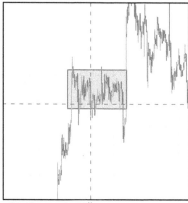

(tradingview.com) Figure 37: Rectangles[xxxviii]
(tradingview.com) Figure 38: Rectangles #2[xxxix]

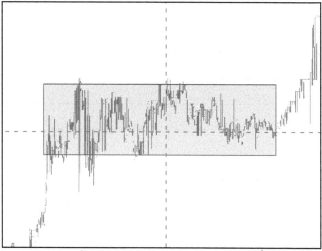

(tradingview.com) Figure 39: Rectangles #3[xl]

WEDGE

Wedge patterns can either be a falling wedge or a rising wedge; falling wedges couple a shrinking price range with a downtrend, while rising wedges combine a shrinking price range with an uptrend. Falling wedges indicate a potential positive breakout while rising wedges signal a negative breakout. While research has shown that both indicators are fairly accurate, the falling wedge is thought to be more reliable than the rising wedge.

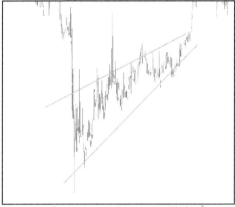

(tradingview.com) Figure 40: Wedge[xli]

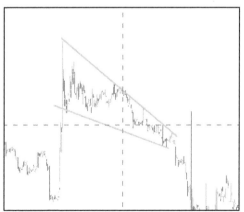

(tradingview.com) Figure 41: Wedge #2[xlii]

HEAD AND SHOULDERS

Head and shoulder patterns are as popular as chart patterns can get; such formations have a reputation for reliability and predict bearish reversals. They involve a baseline price and three peaks, one of which [the head] is sandwiched between the two others [the shoulders]. In concept, this represents a price up trending to a peak, pulling back, accelerating to a new high, pulling back once more, and rising to a third peak before finally succumbing to resistance and falling back below the "neckline" price (formed by the troughs of the first and third peaks) or to support below either shoulder. This completes the reversal. Head and shoulder patterns are often traded upon through an entry at the left-most part of the neckline and a stop-loss above (or below) the estimated price of the right shoulder. That said, while the pattern is known to be reliable (it's found to be correct roughly 85% of the time), it is not a golden rule. As I have previously said, exceptions are necessary to prove a rule.

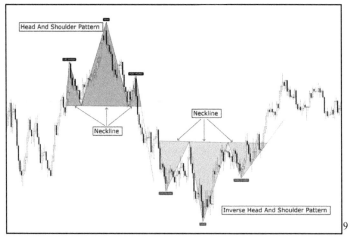

Figure 42: Head and Shoulders[xliii]

INVERSE HEAD AND SHOULDERS

The inverse head and shoulder pattern is the bullish antithesis to the head and shoulder formation. It is also referred to as a "head and shoulders bottom" and consists of a bottom shoulder, a lower head, a subsequent second shoulder, and then a positive breakout above the neckline. The neckline will often switch from resistance to support. To trade upon this formation, investors enter once the neckline price is broken (either immediately after or, to prevent false signals, once the price closes) and sell once the price is run up and finds new resistance.

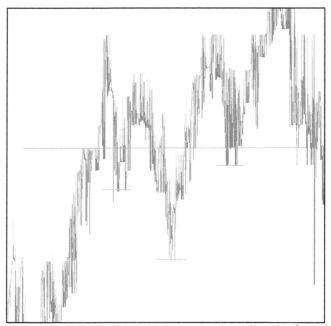

(tradingview.com) Figure 43: Inverse Head and Shoulders[xliv]

DOUBLE BOTTOM/DOUBLE TOP

Double bottoms and double tops are the most common charting patterns. Double tops look like an "M," while double bottoms look like a "W." In each, a price is reached, fallen away from (either positively or negatively), and reached again. Double tops often signify a bearish reversal, while double bottoms can signify bullish reversals. When identifying these patterns, make sure to interpret them carefully and be wary of false signals and similar-looking patterns that aren't actually double bottoms or double tops.

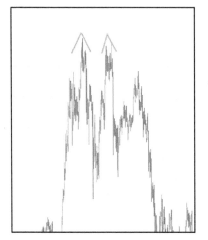 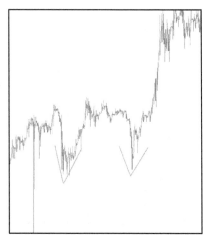

(tradingview.com) Figure 44: Double Top[xlv]
(tradingview.com) Figure 45: Double Bottom[xlvi]

TRIPLE BOTTOM/TRIPLE TOP

The triple top and triple bottom are the next evolution of double tops and double bottoms; they involve a similar price being hit three times and rebounded (either positively or negatively) upon. Triple tops consist of three peaks and pullbacks in between, while triple bottoms consist of three troughs with uptrends in between. Triple tops and triple bottoms are regarded as more reliable than the cousin double bottom and double tops. Triple tops signify bearish reversals, while triple bottoms indicate bullish reversals. Traders can enter short positions once the third peak breakthrough is denied (for triple tops) and long positions once the third trough negative breakthrough is denied (triple bottoms).

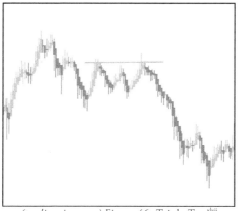

(tradingview.com) Figure 46: Triple Top[xlvii]

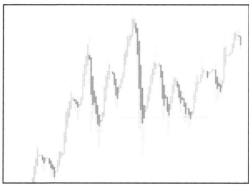

(tradingview.com) Figure 47: Triple Bottom[xlviii]

BUMP AND RUN

Bump and run patterns signal strong reversals, typically subsequent to a fundamentally excessive price increase. The formation consists of three phases: the lead-in, the bump, and the rollover. The lead-in generally lasts either weeks or months and involves a steady uptrend. An angle of 30 to 45 degrees is best (degree measuring tools can be found within most charting services). The bump phase induces a rapid and steep advance in price. Eventually, a top will form. The price then rolls over into a decline that switches previous support levels into resistance levels.

(tradingview.com) Figure 48: Bump and Run[xlix]

COMBINING KNOWLEDGE

To test all of the patterns we have identified, I pulled up a random Bitcoin (BTC) chart and plotted some patterns; price channels, support and resistance, rounded bottoms, triangles, rectangles, and so on (also note that support and resistance often match with nice, round, 10k intervals). I suggest that you do the same with a coin of your choice. This concludes basic chart patterns, and we will now be moving into some specific candlestick formations.

(tradingview.com) Figure 49: Combined Patterns[1]

CANDLESTICK PATTERNS

50 of the most popular and accurate candlestick patterns.

Outline:

- Hammer
- Inverse Hammer
- Hanging Man
- Bullish Engulfing
- Bearish Engulfing
- Piercing Line
- Tweezer Bottom
- Tweezer Top
- Morning Star
- Evening Star
- Three White Soldiers
- Three Black Crows
- Upside Gap Two Crows
- Shooting Star
- Dark Cloud Cover
- Doji
- Marubozu
- Harami
  Harami Cross
- Spinning Top
- Rising Three Methods
- Falling Three Methods
- Abandoned Baby
- Upside Tasuki Gap
- Downside Tasuki Gap
- Piercing Line
- Stick Sandwich
- Three Line Strike
- Two Black Gapping

HAMMER

A hammer is a one-candle pattern that involves a short body with a long lower wick (and little to no upper wick) found at the bottom of a downtrend. Such a sign indicates that strong buying pressure prevented the price from falling further and is likely to drive the price back up.

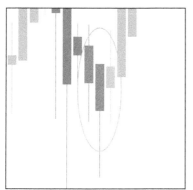

(tradingview.com) Figure 50: Hammer[li]
(tradingview.com) Figure 51: Hammer[lii]

INVERSE HAMMER

An inverse hammer, like a hammer, has a short body at the bottom of a downward trend. However, unlike the hammer, inverse hammers have a long upper wick and a short lower wick. This is still a bullish sign; the bearish hammer equivalent is directly below.

(tradingview.com) Figure 52: Inverse Hammer[liii]
(tradingview.com) Figure 53: Inverse Hammer #2[liv]

HANGING MAN

The hanging man is the bearish equivalent of the hammer. It forms at the end of an uptrend, appears as a short red body with a long lower wick, and is indicative of a downtrend.

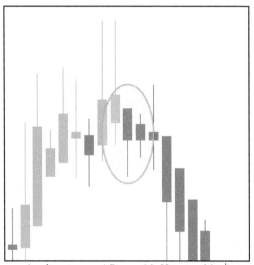

(tradingview.com) Figure 54: Hanging Man[lv]

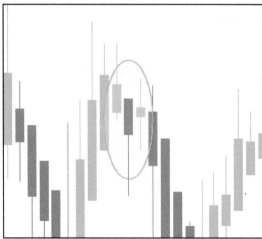

(tradingview.com) Figure 55: Hanging Man #2[lvi]

BULLISH ENGULFING

A bullish engulfing pattern is a two-candle bullish pattern that involves a red candle followed by a green candle that completely covers the first candle (in terms of the body, not the wick). This pattern indicates a positive reversal and occurs less often than may be thought.

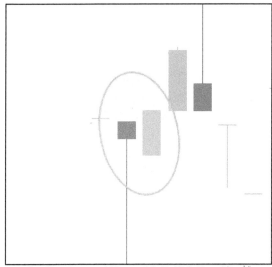

(tradingview.com) Figure 56: Bullish Engulfing[lvii]

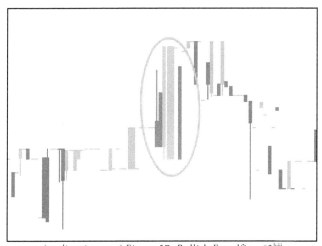

(tradingview.com) Figure 57: Bullish Engulfing #2[lviii]

BEARISH ENGULFING

A bearish engulfing pattern is an uncommon two-candle reversal pattern that involves a small green body engulfed by a subsequent long red body. It indicates an upcoming negative reversal; the lower the second candle goes, the stronger the downtrend is likely to be.

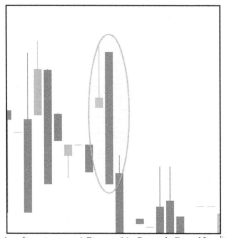

(tradingview.com) Figure 58: Bearish Engulfing[lix]

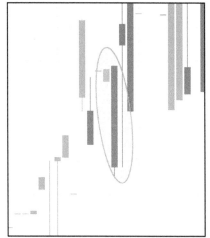

(tradingview.com) Figure 59: Bearish Engulfing[lx]

PIERCING LINE

A piercing line (also called a piercing pattern) is a two-candle pattern that usually follows a price decline. It involves a long red candle with small or no wicks followed by a long green candle that closes above the midpoint of the first candle This indicates heavy buying pressure and a potential positive reversal.

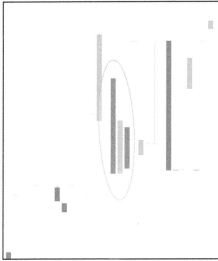

(tradingview.com) Figure 60: Piercing Line[lxi]

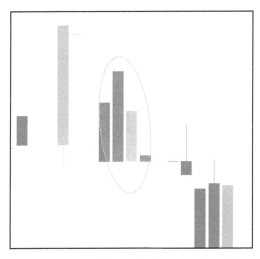

(tradingview.com) Figure 61: Piercing Line #2[lxii]

TWEEZER BOTTOM

A tweezer bottom is a two-candle bullish reversal indicator formed by two consecutive candles, one red and one green, the second of which re-rests the previous low and closes higher. This indicates that the price is unlikely to move lower and may uptrend.

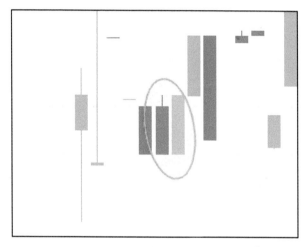

(tradingview.com) Figure 62: Tweezer Bottom[lxiii]

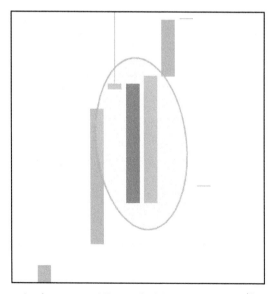

(tradingview.com) Figure 63: Tweezer Bottom #2[lxiv]

TWEEZER TOP

The tweezer top is the bearish opposite of the tweezer bottom. It involves two candles that test a high and close lower, indicated by matching tops. This means that the price is unlikely to move higher and may downtrend.

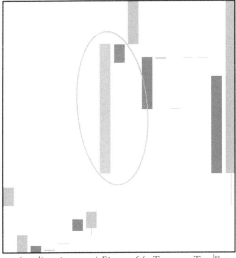

(tradingview.com) Figure 64: Tweezer Top[lxv]

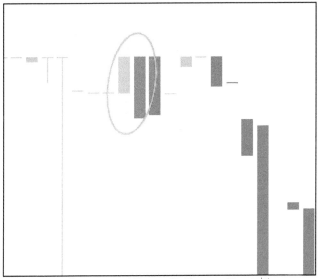

(tradingview.com) Figure 65: Tweezer Top #2[lxvi]

MORNING STAR

The morning star, called such for the hope it brings to traders, is a three-bar pattern that involves a short-bodied candle between a long red and a long green. This indicates that buying pressure is overtaking selling pressure and a positive reversal is likely.

(tradingview.com) Figure 66: Morning Star[lxvii]

EVENING STAR

An evening star is a three-candle bearish reversal pattern that consists of a large green candle followed by a small-body candle (either green or red) that gaps above the previous candle. This is followed by a red candle that closes within the first green body. Such a pattern indicates a downward reversal.

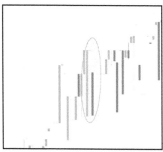 

(tradingview.com) Figure 67: Evening Star #1[lxviii]
(tradingview.com) Figure 68: Evening Star #2[lxix]

THREE WHITE SOLDIERS

Three white soldiers are a very good sign—the trinity involves three consecutive green candles with small wicks. It indicates the end of a downtrend and the beginning of an uptrend.

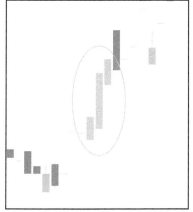 

(tradingview.com) Figure 69: Three White Soldiers[lxx]
(tradingview.com) Figure 70: Three White Soldiers #2[lxxi]

THREE BLACK CROWS

Three black crows are the opposite of three white soldiers—the pattern consists of three consecutive red candles with small wicks. This indicates that the bears have overtaken the bulls and continued downward pressure is probable.

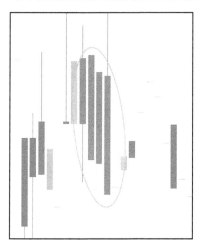 

(tradingview.com) Figure 71: Three Black Crows[lxxii]
(tradingview.com) Figure 72: Three Black Crows #2[lxxiii]

UPSIDE GAP TWO CROWS

The UGTC is a three-candle pattern that signals momentum weakness and a potential negative reversal. It must form in an uptrend and consists of a green candle that pushes the uptrend higher, followed by a red candle that gaps higher at the open, and finally a red candle that opens higher than the second candle and closes below the close of the first green candle. The UGTC should be combined with other indicators or patterns.

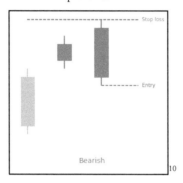

SHOOTING STAR

A shooting star is the opposite of an inverted hammer; it involves a small lower body with a long upper wick (and no lower wick) formed at the top of an uptrend. The upper wick must be at least 2x the length of the body. Shooting stars are bearish and indicate that a higher price was rejected.

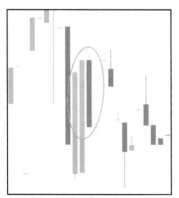

(tradingview.com) Figure 73: Shooting Star[lxxiv]
(tradingview.com) Figure 74: Shooting Star #2[lxxv]

---

[10] *Credit to patternswizard.com/*

DARK CLOUD COVER

Dark cloud cover is a two-candle reversal pattern that forms after an uptrend and consists of a green candle followed by a red candle that closes below the halfway mark of the first candle. This signals that selling pressure overtook previously bullish momentum.

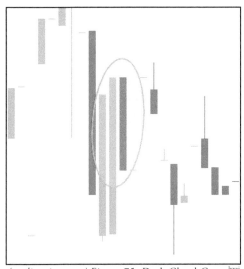

(tradingview.com) Figure 75: Dark Cloud Cover[lxxvi]

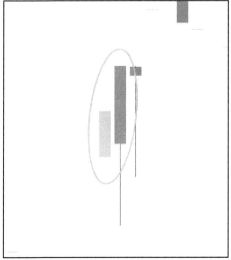

(tradingview.com) Figure 76: Dark Cloud Cover #2[lxxvii]

DOJI

A doji is a very popular type of pattern that forms the basis for quite a few other patterns, many of which are upcoming on this list. Doji candlesticks look like a cross, a plus sign, or an inverted (upside-down) cross. All such patterns are one-candle and indicate probable reversals. All doji patterns open and close within a very small trading range; differentiation occurs within the shadows. Since dojis can come in many different forms, I'd like to fully cover all of the main five doji patterns below, as well as doji stars:

STANDARD DOJI

A standard (neutral) doji forms when opening and closing prices are close to equal. The resulting candle looks like a vertically elongated plus sign.

(tradingview.com) Figure 77: Standard Doji[lxxviii]

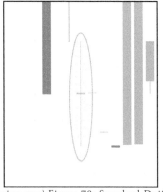

(tradingview.com) Figure 78: Standard Doji #2[lxxix]

LONG-LEGGED DOJI

A long-legged doji is similar to a neutral doji (it is, in fact, a specific kind of a neutral doji), except the wicks are very long, both below and above the body. This indicates indecision since the volume required to reach the highs and lows combined with the small body renders the bears and the bulls practically equal; at the top of an uptrend or the bottom of a downtrend, this can signal a reversal.

(tradingview.com) Figure 79: Long-Legged Doji[lxxx]

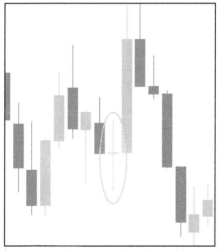

(tradingview.com) Figure 80: Long-Legged Doji #2[lxxxi]

DRAGONFLY DOJI

A dragonfly doji has a small body with a long lower wick and looks like a stretched-out "T." This pattern suggests an imminent reversal and can only form when the opening and closing prices are practically the same and occur at the high of the day. This pattern typically forms at the bottom of a downtrend and signals a potential bullish reversal.

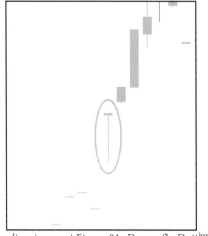

(tradingview.com) Figure 81: Dragonfly Doji[lxxxii]

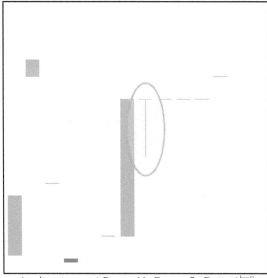

(tradingview.com) Figure 82: Dragonfly Doji #2[lxxxiii]

GRAVESTONE DOJI

A gravestone doji is the opposite of a dragonfly doji; it looks like a flipped "T," or, as the name implies, an elongated tombstone. This pattern typically forms at the top of an uptrend and the long upper shadow suggests a potential downward reversal.

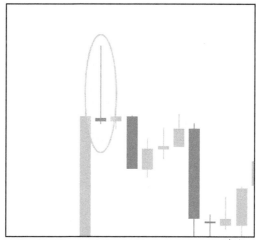

(tradingview.com) Figure 83: Gravestone Doji[lxxxiv]

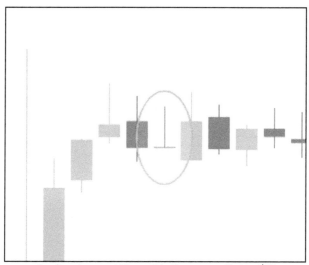

(tradingview.com) Figure 84: Gravestone Doji #2[lxxxv]

FOUR-PRICE DOJI

A four-price (4-price) doji is a rare pattern that occurs when all four prices—open, close, low, and high—are equal. This can really only occur with extreme indecision and low volume.

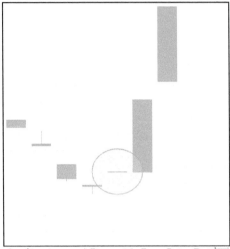

(tradingview.com) Figure 85: Four-Price Doji[lxxxvi]

(tradingview.com) Figure 86: Four-Price Doji #2[lxxxvii]

BULLISH DOJI STAR

Doji stars are a three-candle reversal pattern. The morning doji star is bullish, while the evening doji star is bearish. Morning doji stars form during a downtrend (typically a somewhat long downtrend). They consist of a long-bodied red candle, a second doji-looking candle that gaps lower, and a third candle that closes above the midpoint of the first bar. To minimize risk, a stop-loss can be placed below the second candle.

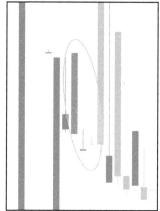

(tradingview.com) Figure 87: Bullish Doji Star[lxxxviii]

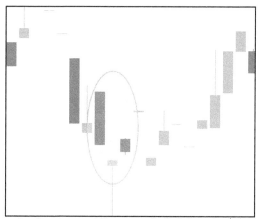

(tradingview.com) Figure 88: Bullish Doji Star[lxxxix]

BEARISH DOJI STAR

The bearish form of a doji star is called the evening doji star; this involves a long-bodied green candle, a second small red candle that looks like a normal doji and gaps above the first candle, and a third bar that closes below the midpoint of the first candle.

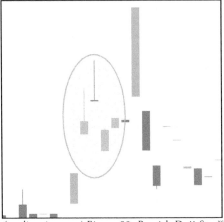

(tradingview.com) Figure 89: Bearish Doji Star[xc]

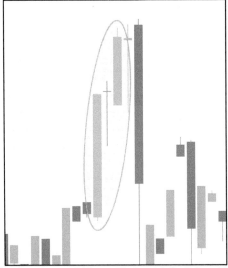

(tradingview.com) Figure 90: Bearish Doji Star #2[xci]

MARUBOZU

Marubozu (also known as the bald/shaven head) is a continuation pattern that consists of one green candle with no to little shadow on either side. A bearish Marubozu constitutes the opposite: one red candle with no or little shadow. Marubozu indicates that a trend is likely to continue.

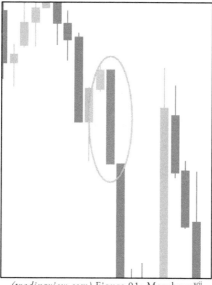

(tradingview.com) Figure 91: Marubozu[xcii]

(tradingview.com) Figure 92: Marubozu #2[xciii]

HARAMI

The harami is a two-candle reversal pattern that comes from the Japanese word "pregnant" which is indicative of the candle's appearance. Haramis can be bearish or bullish; the bullish pattern forms after a downtrend and is made up of one large red candle with small wicks followed by a smaller green candle that gaps up and trades within the open and close of the first {red} candle. The bearish harami pattern is formed by one large green candle, followed by a smaller red candle that gaps up from the previous close and trades within the open and close of the first {green} candle. Both patterns indicate potential reversals; stop-loss orders can be placed at or below the bottom of the first bar.

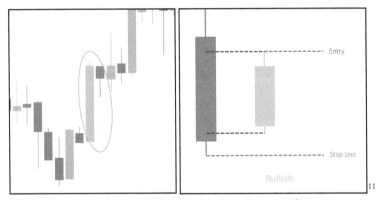

(tradingview.com) Figure 93: Bearish Harami[xciv]
(tradingview.com) Figure 94: Bullish Harami

---

11 *Credit to patternswizard.com*

HARAMI CROSS

A harami cross is a two-candle reversal pattern that combines elements of haramis and dojis. A bullish harami occurs during a downtrend and consists of a large red candle followed by a doji, while a bearish harami occurs during an uptrend and consists of a large green candle followed by a doji. In both the bullish and the bearish patterns, the doji must be contained with the bodies of the first bar. Harami crosses are given more notice if they occur at support levels; this indicates a rebound. As always, Harami crosses, if traded upon, should be used with other indicators and patterns.

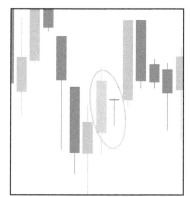 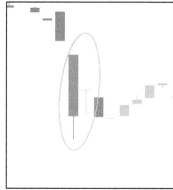

(tradingview.com) Figure 95: Harami Cross[xcv]
(tradingview.com) Figure 96: Harami Cross #2[xcvi]

SPINNING TOP

The spinning top is a one-candle pattern that indicates neither the bulls nor the bears have gained the upper hand. Following a large uptrend or downtrend, this may indicate a reversal; following sideways trading action, this may indicate more neutral movement. Spinning tops consists of a small body vertically centered between long lower and upper shadows. Bullish spinning tops are green candlesticks, while bearish spinning tops are red candlesticks. This pattern can be easily used as a confirming pattern in conjunction with other patterns, oscillators, and indicators.

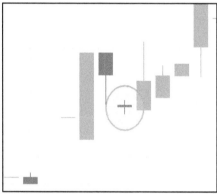

(tradingview.com) Figure 97: Spinning Top[xcvii]

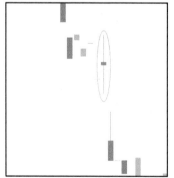

(tradingview.com) Figure 98: Spinning Top #2[xcviii]

RISING THREE METHODS

Rising three methods is a five-candle bullish continuation pattern that, during an uptrend, signals that a trend is likely to continue. The first candle is green with a large body. The next three candles are small, red, and trade within the first candle. The last candle is a large green candle that pushes above the high of the first bar. To manage risk if trading upon this pattern, a stop-loss order can be set slightly beneath the low of the first candle.

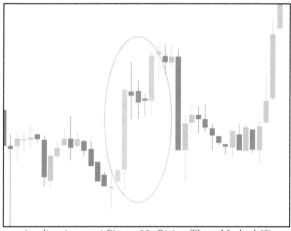

(tradingview.com) Figure 99: Rising Three Methods[xcix]

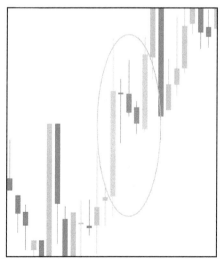

(tradingview.com) Figure 100: Rising Three Methods #2[c]

FALLING THREE METHODS

The falling three methods is the bearish equivalent of the rising three methods (left) that indicates a likely continuation of previous trends. The first candle is a large and red, followed by three small green bars that trade within the first candle. The last candle is large, red, and breaks below the low set by the first candle. As with the rising three methods, a stop-loss order can be placed slightly above the high of the first candle to manage risk while shorting.

(tradingview.com) Figure 101: Falling Three Methods[ci]

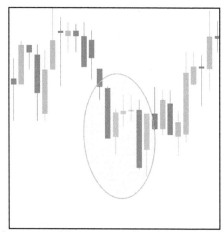

(tradingview.com) Figure 102: Falling Three Methods #2[cii]

ABANDONED BABY

The abandoned baby is a rare three-bar reversal pattern known to be quite reliable in identifying short-term reversals, especially after rapid price drops or rises. It's similar to the morning star and evening star formations and can be either bullish or bearish; the bearish pattern is predictive of an uptrend reversal and forms when a large-bodied green candle is followed by a doji candle that gaps upwards and a third large-bodied red candle that gaps downwards. The first and the third candles typically have small shadows. The bullish equivalent, predictive of a downtrend reversal, consists of a large green candle, a doji that gaps lower, and a third large green candle that gaps higher. I must note, I could not find the origin of the name, but I can say that the original Japanese term for the pattern, "sute go," translates to "child abandonment," so the term has been around for some time.

(tradingview.com) Figure 103: Abandoned Baby[ciii]
(tradingview.com) Figure 104: Abandoned Baby #2[civ]

UPSIDE TASUKI GAP

The upside tasuki gap is a three-bar continuation pattern that involves a large green candle, a subsequent green candle that gaps above the high of the previous candle, and a third red candle that closes between the gap of the proceeding two candles. The third candle indicates that resistance was shortly met but didn't last; hence, the uptrend should continue.

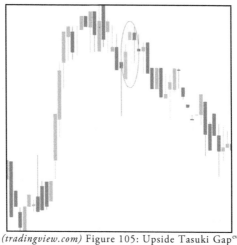

(tradingview.com) Figure 105: Upside Tasuki Gap[cv]

(tradingview.com) Figure 106: Upside Tasuki Gap #2[cvi]

DOWNSIDE TASUKI GAP

The downside tasuki gap is the opposite of the upside tasuki gap (above). It is formed by a large red candle, a second red candle that gaps below the close of the first candle, and a third green candle that closes within the gap of the first two bars.

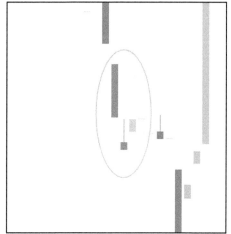

(tradingview.com) Figure 107: Downside Tasuki Gap[cvii]

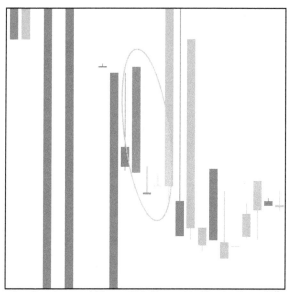

(tradingview.com) Figure 108: Downside Tasuki Gap #2[cviii]

PIERCING LINE

The piercing line is a two-candle bullish reversal pattern that follows a downtrend. The first candle is red, and the second green candle must close above the midline of the first [red] bar. This indicates a positive reversal.

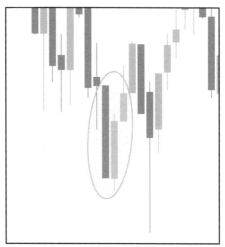

(tradingview.com) Figure 109: Piercing Line[cix]

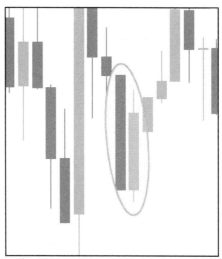

(tradingview.com) Figure 110: Piercing Line #2[cx]

TWO BLACK GAPPING

Two black gapping is a bearish continuation pattern that appears after an uptrend and consists of a gap followed by two red candles, each forming lower lows. It indicates that the price will continue downtrending.

(tradingview.com) Figure 111: Two Black Gapping[cxi]

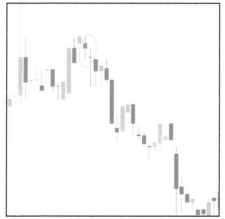

(tradingview.com) Figure 112: Two Black Gapping #2[cxii]

STICK SANDWICH

Stick sandwiches are rare three-candle reversal patterns that can be either bearish or bullish. As the name implies, this pattern looks like a sandwich. Bullish patterns consist of one small green candle sandwiched between two larger red candles, the first of which closes near its low. The second green candle gaps up from the previous close and closes above the previous candle open. The last candle has the same closing price as the first candle. Following this pattern, an uptrend is likely to occur if the high of the third candle is broken. The opposite of this [a bearish stick sandwich] involves a large green candle that closes near its high, a second red candle that gaps downward and closes between the previous candle open, and a final green candle that has the same closing price as the first candle. Once the low of the third candle is broken, a downtrend is likely to occur or continue.

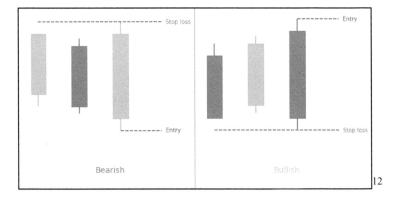

12

THREE LINE STRIKE

The three-line strike is a rare bullish or bearish five-candle reversal pattern. The bullish pattern is made up of a large green candle, three subsequent green candles, and a large red candle, of which the low is lower than the prior three candles (not all four). This indicates that an uptrend will continue. The bearish three-line strike pattern consists of three red candles followed by a large green candle that brings the price above the high of the previous three bearish candles. To manage risk within the three-line strike, a trailing stop-loss can be applied.

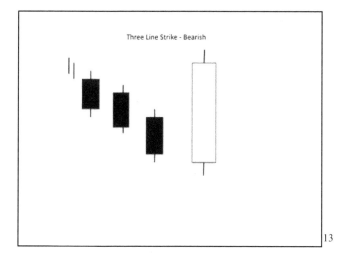

13

13 Credit to avasaram.com

ESSENTIAL: PATTERNS

This essentials section consists of a simplified view of eight patterns out of the fifty or so above. All are important, and modern charting tools allow for patterns such as these to be automatically and easily identified.

The following patterns made it to this list:

1. Triangles
2. Rectangles
3. Head and Shoulders
4. Double/Triple Bottom/Top
5. Doji
6. Morning Star/Evening Star
7. Abandoned Baby
8. Two Black Gapping

TRIANGLES

Triangle patterns can be either symmetrical, ascending, or descending. Ascending triangles consist of a horizontal trendline and a diagonally rising lower trendline, descending triangles consist of a horizontal lower trendline and a diagonally sinking upper trendline, and symmetrical triangles represent two trend lines and a shrinking price range. Ascending triangles signal bullish breakouts, descending triangles signal bearish breakouts, and symmetrical triangles signal breakouts in either direction.

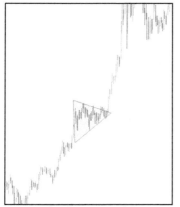 

(tradingview.com) Figure 113: Symmetrical Triangle #3[cxiii]
(tradingview.com) Figure 114: Symmetrical Triangle #4[cxiv]

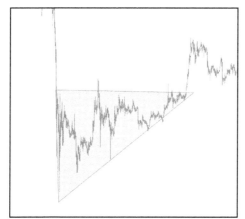

(tradingview.com) Figure 115: Ascending Triangle #3[cxv]

RECTANGLES

Rectangle formations are continuation patterns signified by near-equal successive tops and bottoms. Rectangles have been found to be roughly 80% accurate, and breakouts reliably extend as far as the trading range (the width) of the rectangle.

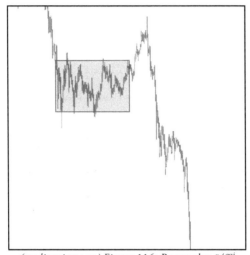

(tradingview.com) Figure 116: Rectangles #4[cxvi]

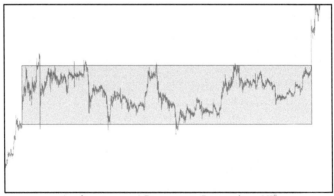

(tradingview.com) Figure 117: Rectangles #5[cxvii]

*Note that the resulting uptrends in both cases were roughly equivalent to the height of the respective rectangles.

HEAD AND SHOULDERS

Head and shoulders are statistically the most accurate price action pattern and are correct roughly 85% of the time. The pattern consists of a baseline price and three peaks; the middle peak is called the "head" and is sandwiched between two "shoulders." The troughs of the shoulders form the "neckline" price. Head and shoulder formations indicate a bearish reversal. Inverse head and shoulder patterns are bullish.

(tradingview.com) Figure 118: Inverse Head and Shoulders #2[ccviii]

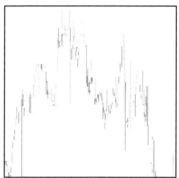

(tradingview.com) Figure 119: Head and Shoulders #2[ccix]

DOUBLE/TRIPLE BOTTOM/TOP

Double tops, double bottoms, triple tops, and triple bottoms signify reversals. Each is signified by the corresponding number of distinct peaks or troughs. The formations, as a whole, are 75% to 80% accurate.

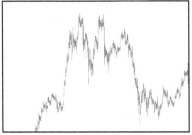 

(tradingview.com) Figure 120: Double Top #2[cxx]
(tradingview.com) Figure 121: Triple Bottom #3[cxxi]

(tradingview.com) Figure 122: Double Top #3[cxxii]

DOJI

Dojis are one-candle formations characterized by a small trading range and long shadows. Standard dojis and long-legged dojis have shadows of equal length, dragonfly dojis have long lower shadows, gravestone dojis have long upper shadows, and four-price dojis are one thin, horizontal line with no shadows. Dojis often signify reversals but are much better used in conjunction with other bars to form more reliable indicators.

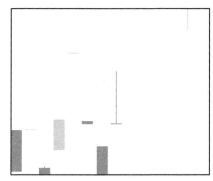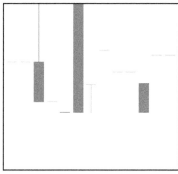

(tradingview.com) Figure 123: Gravestone Doji #3[cxxiii]
(tradingview.com) Figure 124: Dragonfly Doji #3[cxxiv]

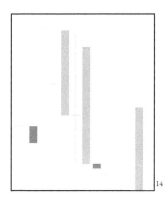

(tradingview.com) Figure 125: Long-Legged (Neutral) Doji[cxxv]

---

[14] *Four price dojis are located in all three images.

MORNING STAR/EVENING STAR

The morning star and evening star are three-bar patterns. Morning is bullish and evening is bearish. The morning star constitutes a short-bodied candle between a long red (left) and a long green (right). The evening star constitutes a long green (left), a short-bodied middle candle, and a long red (right). Morning stars happen at the bottom of a downtrend, while evening stars happen at the top of uptrends. Both indicate reversals.

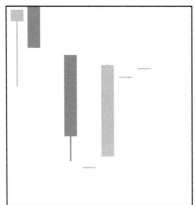 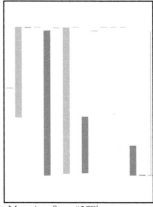

(tradingview.com) Figure 126: Morning Star #2[cxxvi]
(tradingview.com) Figure 127: Morning Star #3[cxxvii]

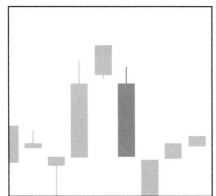

(tradingview.com) Figure 128: Evening Star #3[cxxviii]

ABANDONED BABY

An abandoned baby is a three-bar reversal pattern. The bullish pattern constitutes a large candle, a doji that gaps lower, and a third large green candle that gaps higher. The bearish equivalent constitutes a large green candle followed by a doji that gaps upwards and, finally, a large-bodied red candle that gaps downward. This formation is known to be apt at marking short-term reversals.

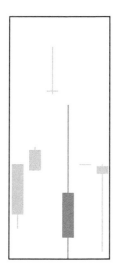
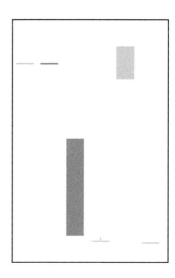

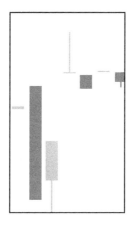

(tradingview.com) Figure 129: Abandoned Baby[cxxix]
(tradingview.com) Figure 130: Abandoned Baby #2[cxxx]
(tradingview.com) Figure 131: Abandoned Baby #3[cxxxi]

TWO BLACK GAPPING

Two black gapping is a bearish continuation pattern that constitutes two red candles formed at the top of an uptrend, the second of which gaps below the first. This is indicative that the short-term trend will remain bearish. This formation is accurate roughly 70% of the time.

(tradingview.com) Figure 132: Two Black Gapping #3[cxxxii]
(tradingview.com) Figure 133: Two Black Gapping #4[cxxxiii]

(tradingview.com) Figure 134: Two Black Gapping #5[cxxxiv]

INDICATORS

This section covers a few select indicators not covered in either the oscillator or the pattern section.

ICHIMOKU (KINKO HYO)/ICHIMOKU CLOUD

The Ichimoku is a popular tool that combines momentum, trend, support, and resistance into one indicator. The indicator can seem intimidating; however, if time is taken to understand the Ichimoku, the result can be a streamlined and efficient analysis process. The five lines of the Ichimoku combine to form an "Ichimoku cloud," which collapses the information from all five lines into one easier-to-read formation. The five lines that form the Ichimoku cloud are also viewable while using the Ichimoku, hence providing the dexterity and multi-faceted approach that the Ichimoku is known for.

Baseline - Tenkan-Sen

The Tenkan-Sen is a moving average that is typically represented as a red line. It indicates a general market trend (upwards, downwards, or sideways).

Conversion Line - Kijun-Sen

The Kijun-Sen acts as support and resistance and is typically represented by a blue line. The Kijun-Sen is similar to the Tenkan-Sen, except a longer time frame is applied. Hence, the Kijun usually lags the Tenkan.

Leading Span A - Senkou A

The Senkou A is the average of the highs and lows of the previous two lines [Tenkan-Sen and Kijun-Sen], and is typically represented as an orange line. If the price of the coin or token is above the value of the Senkou A, the top and bottom lines [of the five] become support levels, while if the price moves below the Senkou span A, the bottom and top lines become resistance.

Leading Span B - Senkou B

Senkou span B is an expanded version of Senkou A. The difference between Senkou A and Senkou B is colored and creates the Ichimoku cloud; if the Senkou A is above the Senkou B, the cloud is green. If the Senkou A is below the Senkou B, the cloud is red.

Lagging Span - Chikou Span

The Chikou span shifts the current price 26 periods leftward and is represented as a green line. When the Chikou span crosses the price in an upwards direction, it indicates a buy signal, and a Chikou span cross below the price is a sell signal.

Ichimoku Signals

- When the Tenkan-Sen and Kijun-Sen are above the cloud , the trend is positive.
- When the Tenkan-Sen and Kijun-Sen are below the cloud, the trend is negative.
- A buy signal is reinforced when the Tenkan-Sen crosses above the Kijun-Sen while both lines and the price is above the cloud.
- A sell signal is reinforced when the Tenkan-Sen crosses below the Kijun-Sen when both lines and the price are above the cloud.

The Ichimoku Cloud is often paired with momentum indicators, such as the RSI and Stochastic oscillator.

BOLLINGER BANDS

Bollinger bands are a simple indicator known as a price envelope. Price envelopes are displayed as a band around a price and identify range, support, and resistance. Through identifying range, traders can get an idea of whether prices are high or low on a relative basis. Bollinger bands are used in conjunction with a moving average, which is a line called the "middle band" that stays roughly within the upper and lower band. The closer the price hugs either the upper or lower band, the stronger the trend is, and the closer the price to the upper band, the more overbought the price, while the closer the price moves to the lower band, the more oversold the price. Since approximately 90% of price action occurs between the two bands, the resulting 10% of price action is likely to be major breakouts. Stop losses can be placed at the breakout price once the breakout is confirmed.

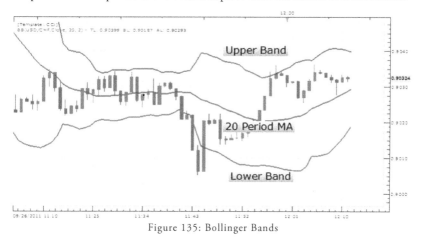

Figure 135: Bollinger Bands

BOLLINGER BAND WIDTH (BBW)

The Bollinger band width is the difference between the upper and lower bands divided by the middle band. The BBW is portrayed as one single line. Higher BBW values indicate a more overbought condition, while lower BBW values indicate a more oversold condition.

PARABOLIC SAR

The Parabolic SAR (stop and reverse) is an indicator created by J. Welles Wilder[15] to determine trend direction and identify reversals. On a chart, this indicator appears as a series of dots. Dots below the price are bullish, while dots above the price are bearish. Dots that cross price signal a trend reversal. Parabolic SARs work best during a strongly trending market, as opposed to a choppy or sideways-trading market. The Parabolic SAR is best used in combination with another indicator that can determine the strength of trends instead of the occurrence thereof.

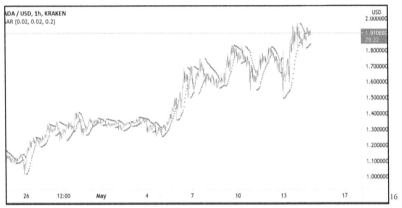

Figure 136: Parabolic SAR

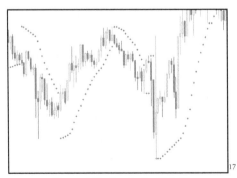

Figure 137: Parabolic SAR #2

---

[15] Wilder also created the RSI.
[16] Original image.
[17] Original image.

GANN

William Delbert Gann (1878−1955) was a finance trader known for using time cycles, geometry, and other forms of mathematics to predict events in price action. Here are a few rules[18] from W. D. Gann:[19]

- Always use stop-loss orders.
- Reduce trading after your first loss; don't increase (this is also mentioned further on in the trading rules section).
- Don't buy or sell just because a price is low or high.
- Don't overtrade.
- Don't alter a position without a good reason.

GANN FAN

Gann angles are tools based upon the idea of the market being cyclical, and of time affecting price. Gann fans consist of lines that incorporate ratios to determine angles. The ratios are 1:8, 1:4, 1:3, 1:2, 1:1, 2:1, 3:1, 4:1, and 8:1. All base themselves off of a central 45-degree angle (meaning the 45-degree line is the 1:1). The 1:1 line is regarded as the main indicator of support and resistance and the other lines also serve as lesser support and resistance indicators. The 1:1 line should always be placed on the chart at a 45-degree angle. Below are the angles of all 9 Gann fan lines assuming the ratios prescribed above.

1 x 8 = 82.5 degrees	1 x 4 = 75 degrees	1 x 3 = 71.25 degrees
1 x 2 = 63.75 degrees	1 x 1 = 45 degrees	2 x 1 = 26.25 degrees
3 x 1 = 18.75 degrees	4 x 1 = 15 degrees	8 x 1 = 7.5 degrees

---

[18] He also has some unconventional rules, including these:

- If the market rises for 5 consecutive days, it is likely that a correction will last for 3 days.

- In a highly uptrending market, weekly lows happen on Tuesday.

- In a strongly downtrending market, weekly highs are usually achieved on Wednesday.

[19] These rules were written specifically in regard to the stock market, but still hold relevancy to cryptocurrencies.

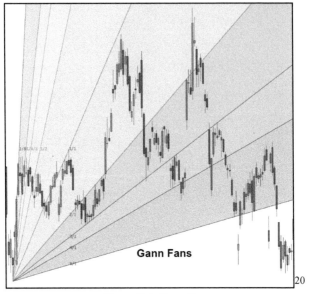

Figure 138: Gann Fan
Note the ratios.

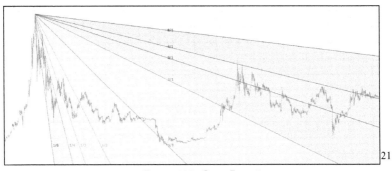

Figure 139: Gann Fan #2
Note the plotted lines, especially the 4/1, forming support and resistance for price.

---

20 *Credit to Investopedia.com*
21 *Credit to patternswizard.com*

PITCHFORK

The standard pitchfork indicator, known as Andrews' Pitchfork, is a tool that allows for quick identification of support and resistance through trend channels. Pitchforks are created through three points on the chart, all of which are placed at the end of previous trends. Lines extend diagonally upward from the three points, forming a pitchfork pattern. This creates the "median line" and another two sets of lines above and below that median line. The below chart shows how the pitchfork lines act as support and resistance in the upper right portion of the chart. Pitchfork upper and lower line breakout should be confirmed through other indicators that can judge trend strength (and the likeness of a breakout) instead of just where that breakout should occur.

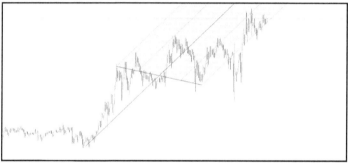

(tradingview.com) Figure 140: Andrews' Pitchfork (chart)

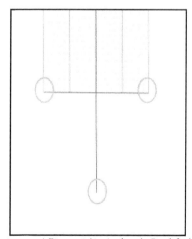

(tradingview.com) Figure 141: Andrew's Pitchfork (visual)

SCHIFF PITCHFORK

The Schiff Pitchfork is derived from Andrews' Pitchfork; the difference is in the location of the origin point, which is ½ of the vertical distance between the high and low points.

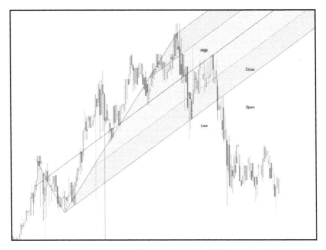

(tradingview.com) Figure 142: Schiff Pitchfork[cxxxv]

FIBONACCI

You may have heard of Fibonacci numbers, the golden rule, or the Fibonacci sequence. Fibonacci numbers and tools fill a top spot in the indicator market and maintain a cult-like following. The Fibonacci sequence was invented by Leonardo of Pisa[22] (1180–1250), an Italian who grew up in North Africa during the Middle Ages. His nickname was Fibonacci. He wrote a work called "Libre Abaci," which roughly translates to "The Book of Calculation." The book popularized the Hindu-Arabic arithmetic system relative to the old Roman numeral system. Within the book, the sequence of numbers that later became the Fibonacci sequence[23] was used to calculate the growth of a rabbit population. The question was this: How many pairs of rabbits will there be in one year, assuming that one initial pair of rabbits produces another pair of rabbits every month following a one-month infertility period? (each pair breeds indefinitely.) The result is an equation that adds the sum of the two previous terms to get the next term:

$$F(n) = F(n) + F(n-1)$$

So, starting with 1 pair of rabbits, the following would ensue:

1 + 0 = 1[24]	0 + 1 = 1	1 + 1 = 2	1+ 2 = 3	2 + 3 = 5	5 + 3 = 8
8 + 5 = 13	8 + 13 = 21	13 + 21 = 34	21 + 34 = 55	34 + 55 = 89	55 + 89 = 144

---

[22] His name may also be Leonardo Fibonacci, Leonardo Bonacci, or Leonardo Pisano.
[23] Fibonacci himself didn't regard his calculations as important. Instead, in 1877, the mathematician Edouard Lucas published studies involving the sequence which he called "the Fibonacci Sequence" in honor of the original author.
[24] The initial pair of rabbits is infertile for the first month, hence the repeated 1.

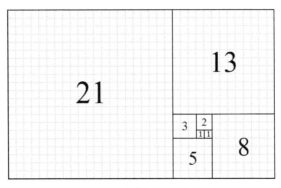

Figure 143: Golden Numbers[cxxxvi]

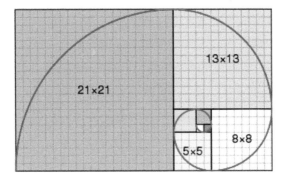

Figure 144: Fibonacci Spiral[cxxxvii]

The resulting sequence and the equation (the summing the previous two terms) is called the Fibonacci sequence. The golden spiral (bottom picture) is derived from the Fibonacci sequence. Both pictures involve the "golden ratio" of 1.618. Upon further research, the Fibonacci sequence and the golden ratio have been found all over the natural world and have proven to be a naturally occurring pattern. Such patterns can be found in pinecones, flowers, various fruits and vegetables, honeybee colonies, and even the human body.

Fibonacci numbers have since been found to hold sway in the stock market. All Fibonacci market-related tools involve a trendline (often multiple) drawn between two points and indicate support and resistance.

FIBONACCI RETRACEMENT

The Fibonacci retracement tool plots retracement lines as per the Fibonacci sequence. A retracement is a minor pullback or change in direction, so a retracement line is a line that indicates where support and resistance (hence, pullbacks and change in direction) are likely to occur. Fibonacci retracements are created by drawing a trend line between two points (typically a low and a high, or vice versa). Six horizontal lines are then automatically drawn at points that intersect the original trend line. These interception points occur at Fibonacci levels of 0.0%, 23.6%, 38.2%, 50%, 61.8%, and 100% (in fraction form: 1, 0.786, 0.618, 0.5 0.382, 0.236, and 0). These lines identify possible areas of support and resistance.

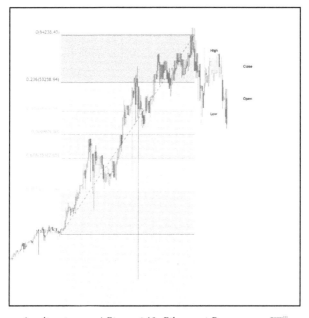

(tradingview.com) Figure 145: Fibonacci Retracement[cxxxviii]

FIBONACCI FANS

Fibonacci fan lines are similar to the Fibonacci retracement. First, a trend line is drawn between two points (typically an extreme point—either a high or a low). Then, four trend lines are drawn from the initial point and pass through an invisible vertical line below the second extreme point at the Fibonacci percentage levels described previously.

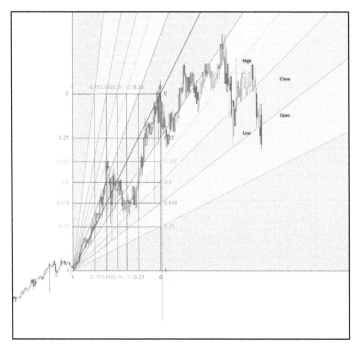

(tradingview.com) Figure 146: Fibonacci Fans

FIBONACCI ARCS

Fibonacci arcs are half-circles that extend outward from a vertical line that extends from the second of the two extreme points. The arcs of the half-circle are drawn at points that interest the trend line at Fibonacci levels.

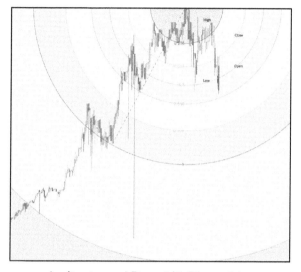

(tradingview.com) Figure 147: Fibonacci Arcs

Other Fibonacci Tools:

Fib Wedge - set of Fibonacci-based arcs.

Fib Channel - parallel Fibonacci-based trendlines.

Fib Circles - 11-layered Fibonacci-based circle.

Fib Time Zones - vertical lines that represent potential movement based on Fibonacci-based time increments.

MOVING AVERAGE (MA)

Moving averages are lagging indicators that signal support, resistance, and momentum through a singular, smoothed-out line (this line serves as support and resistance) calculated in partnership with a time frame. Hence, one may say "5-day MA" or 100-day MA." Often, moving averages are used in pairs; in such cases, crossovers signal change in momentum (positive if the shorter-term MA crosses above the longer-term MA and negative if the shorter-term MA falls below the longer-term MA). Exponential moving averages (EMAs) are MAs that place greater importance on recent price action, hence creating a signal line that associates more closely with price.

Figure 148: Moving Averages[25]

---

[25] Credit to dailyfx.com

OSCILLATORS

Oscillators, to recap, construct an upper and lower limit and provide a number that fluctuates within these bounds. I'll quickly note that they're pronounced "awe-si-laters"—the c is silent. Typically, the high limit represents an overbought condition, while the low limit represents an oversold condition (limits are typically multiples of 10). Therefore, the higher the line, the more of a sell it is, and the lower the line, the more a buy it is. We will cover 15 oscillators , all of which are loosely ranked in order of popularity:

- Relative Strength Index (RSI)
- Moving Average Convergence Divergence (MACD)
- Stochastic Oscillator
- True Strength Index (TSI)
- Money Flow Index (MSI)
- Commodity Channel Index (CCI)
- Klinger Oscillator (KO)
- Percentage Price Oscillator (PPO)
- Percentage Volume Oscillator (PVO)
- Chaikin Oscillator (CO)
- SMI Ergodic Oscillator (SMIEO)
- Detrended Price Oscillator (DPO)
- Chande Momentum Oscillator (CMO)
- Ultimate Oscillator (UO)
- Awesome Oscillator (AO)

I ask you to make this an involved process. I chose only to show graphs of each oscillator, and not the graph the oscillator is based upon, to save space. However, it is a much better experience if you pull up free charts and experiment with each oscillator while simultaneously viewing the graph.

RELATIVE STRENGTH INDEX (RSI)

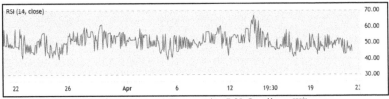

(tradingview.com) Figure 149: RSI Oscillator[cxxxix]

The RSI, originally developed by J. Welles Wilder Jr. in 1978, is a momentum oscillator that measures the strength or weakness of price trends. The RSI trades within a range of 0 to 100; a value over 70 indicates an overbought condition and suggests an incoming pullback, while a value under 30 indicates an oversold condition and suggests an upward reversal. To simplify: higher is bearish, while lower is bullish. In the chart below, the red circles indicate overbought conditions (and hence, sell signals), while the green circles indicate oversold conditions (buy signals).

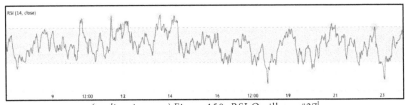

(tradingview.com) Figure 150: RSI Oscillator #2[cxl]

MOVING AVERAGE CONVERGENCE DIVERGENCE (MACD)

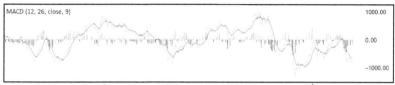

(tradingview.com) Figure 151: MACD Oscillator[cxli]

The MACD is a popular (if not the most popular) momentum oscillator used to identify price trends. MACD charts contain two lines (above, the blue and yellow line) and a histogram. The two lines are the MACD and a signal line. The MACD is found by subtracting the 26-day EMA from the 12-day EMA and the signal line is a 9-day EMA. Crossovers between these two lines indicate either a bearish move or a bullish move—bullish when the MACD crosses above the signal line, and bearish when the MACD passes below the signal line. MACD charts also display a histogram (which looks similar to volume, but it isn't). The histogram displays the distance between the MACD and the signal line. If the MACD is above the signal line (remember, a bullish move), the histogram is above baseline, as represented in green. If the MACD is below the signal line, the histogram is below baseline, in red. The height of the histogram indicates the strength or weakness of the trend and the probability of a reversal. The MACD is often combined with the RSI (directly above), which provides a more thorough look at overbought/oversold conditions and momentum. In the chart below, note the crossovers (bullish in green and bearish in red) and note how deviation on the histogram provides information on trend strength.

(tradingview.com) Figure 152: MACD Oscillator #2[cxlii]

STOCHASTIC OSCILLATOR (SO)

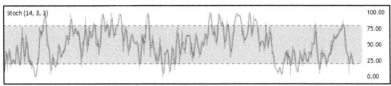

(tradingview.com) Figure 153: Stochastic Oscillator[cxliii]

The Stochastic Oscillator is another momentum indicator developed in the 1950s by George Lane that, like the RSI, oscillates within a range of 0 to 100. The SO generates information on overbought versus oversold conditions. Since it doesn't rely on price or volume, just speed and momentum, the stochastic is a leading indicator to predict trends and reversals before they happen This works because changes in momentum often foreshadow trends before those trends happen. Similar to the RSI, the stochastic uses a range to indicate overbought and oversold conditions, which functions exactly the same as the 70/30 on the RSI but happens to be 80 and 20. Several variations of the stochastic oscillator are used: the fast stochastic, which is choppier and more volatile; the slow stochastic, which is smoothed with an SMA; and the full stochastic, as shown in the above and below visuals.

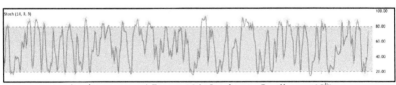

(tradingview.com) Figure 154: Stochastic Oscillator #2[cxliv]

TRUE STRENGTH INDEX (TSI)

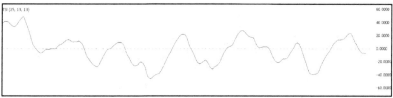

(tradingview.com) Figure 155: TSI Oscillator[cxlv]

The True Strength Index is a momentum oscillator created in 1991 by William Blau. The TSI can be used to identify buying and selling pressure (meaning the same as overbought and oversold levels), as well as the strength and duration of trends. The TSI is based around a centerline (dotted). A positive value (anything above the centerline line) indicates positive momentum, while a negative value indicates negative momentum. The other two lines within the TSI graph are similar to the MACD: one is the signal line, and the other is the TSI indicator. When the TSI crosses under the signal line, it forecasts a bearish trend, while the TSI crossing over the signal line is bullish. So, crossovers are a great way to use the TSI, and another is to view the overbought and oversold levels, which vary by asset. You can determine these levels by looking to see what values (say, +30, +20, or +15) historically led to a pullback and vice versa. Divergence is also an important concept within the TSI. Divergence is the degree of separation between the price and the indicator. For example, divergence would be exemplified if the TSI drops heavily while the price moves upwards. A bullish divergence occurs when the price is dropping while the TSI is rising, and bearish divergence occurs when the price is rising while the TSI is dropping.

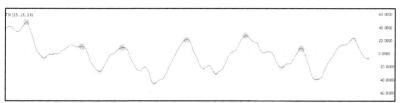

(tradingview.com) Figure 156: TSI Oscillator #2[cxlvi]

MONEY FLOW INDEX (MFI)

(tradingview.com) Figure 157: MFI Oscillator[cdvii]

The Money Flow Index is a technical oscillator that measures overbought or oversold conditions through a combination of price and volume. The MFI may also be called the volume-weighted RSI because the two use the same base formula and differ only through the incorporation of volume. A value over 80 indicates an overbought price, while a value under 20 indicates an oversold price. To omit false signals, some traders prefer using an upper limit of 90 and a lower limit of 10. Price movement can also be predicted through divergence, as in the TSI (left). It's a bad sign if the price is moving up and the MFI is moving down, while if the price is moving down and the MFI is moving up, it is a good sign. The MFI is best used in combination with another momentum indicator, such as the RSI and TSI.

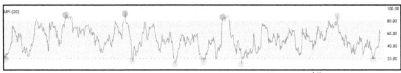

(tradingview.com) Figure 158: MFI Oscillator #2[cdviii]

COMMODITY CHANNEL INDEX (CCI)

(tradingview.com) Figure 159: CCI Oscillator[cxlix]

The CCI is a lagging momentum oscillator developed by Donald Lambert in 1980 to signal overbought and oversold levels by measuring the difference between current and historical prices. The CCI has no set limits (such as the "0" and "100" within the RSI) and is called an unbounded oscillator. For this reason, overbought/oversold conditions are identified and altered based only on historical data. Normally, these conditions are identified when outside a +100 or -100 range. So, a value over 100 indicates an overbought condition, while a value under -100 indicates an oversold condition. The CCI was originally intended to generate buy and sell signals when +100/-100 bounds were exceeded and then traded when the value peaked and reversals seemed imminent. Keep in mind that although it is generally accurate, it is a lagging indicator, so it may miss trends. The CCI is best used alongside trend lines and moving averages.

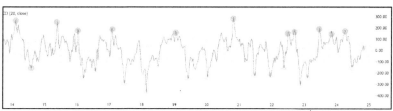

(tradingview.com) Figure 160: CCI Oscillator #2[cl]

KLINGER OSCILLATOR (KO)

(tradingview.com) Figure 161: KO Oscillator[di]

The Klinger Oscillator is a simplistic volume indicator created by Stephen J. Klinger that specializes in identifying long-term money flow trends (while still remaining predictive of short-term moves). It works by comparing volume (volume force) to price movement (EMAs) and then simplifying the results into an oscillator that fluctuates below and above zero. The two lines, typically red and blue, can be used as signals either during centerline crosses (crossing zero) or crossovers. A crossover above the signal line is a bullish indicator, while a crossover below the signal line is a bearish indicator. Divergence should be noted; it is good if the Klinger is positive, but the price is falling, and not good if vice versa. Given the many false signals it may incur, it is best combined (based upon Al Hill's research) with the stochastic oscillator, parabolic SAR, and/or two moving averages.

(tradingview.com) Figure 162: KO Oscillator #2[26]

---

[26] Highlighted buying and selling signals are applied only for effect. The red and green dots on the chart already display the crossovers.

PERCENTAGE PRICE OSCILLATOR (PPO)

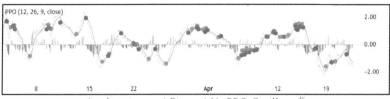

(tradingview.com) Figure 163: PPO Oscillator[clii]

The PPO is a momentum indicator similar to the MACD, except the MACD measures the absolute difference between two EMAs, while the PPO measures the percentage difference. This renders the PPO comparable between multiple assets with different absolute prices, as opposed to the MACD. Like the MACD, the PPO generates buy signals through crossovers. When the PPO line crosses above the signal line, it is a buy, and when it crosses below the signal line, it is a sell. The two lines relative to the centerline are important; above zero is considered bullish, while below zero is considered bearish. The histogram displays divergence (the distance between the PPO and the signal line).

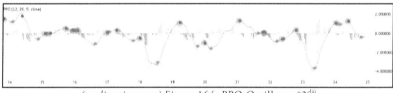

(tradingview.com) Figure 164: PPO Oscillator #2[cliii]

PERCENTAGE VOLUME OSCILLATOR (PVO)

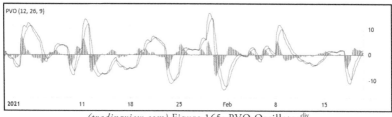

(tradingview.com) Figure 165: PVO Oscillator[div]

The PVO is a momentum oscillator; as with the MACD, the PVO is represented as a centerline, two lines (one, the PVO, and the second, the signal line), and a histogram. Crossovers between the signal line, which is a 9-day EMA of the PVO, and the PVO; which is a 12-day volume EMA (VEMA) subtracted from a 26-day VEMA divided by the longer VEMA period multiplied by 100, are used as confirming indicators to support breakout signals. Centerline crossovers indicate that, if above zero, volume is above average, and, if below zero, volume is below average. As with the MACD, the PVO's histogram represents divergence. The PVO must is best used with one or multiple supporting indicator.

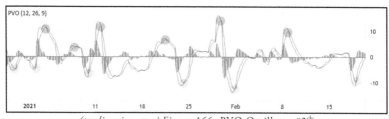

(tradingview.com) Figure 166: PVO Oscillator #2[clv]

CHAIKIN OSCILLATOR (CO)

(tradingview.com) Figure 167: CO Oscillator[clvi]

The Chaikin Oscillator, created by Marc Chaikin (founder of Chaikin Analytics), measures the momentum of the accumulation-distribution line (the ADL is an indicator that measures underlying supply and demand) of the MACD. It is a leading indicator designed to predict momentum and price trends. The ADL is represented as the centerline in Chaikin graphs, and the value (the line) is found by subtracting 10-day and 3-day EMAs. Buy and sell signals are generated with centerline crossovers over the ADL (buy) and centerline crossovers under the ADL (sell). Additionally, positive divergence (meaning the oscillator is moving up while the price is moving down) signals an uptrend, and a rising price combined with a falling oscillator signals a downtrend. You may also trade according to a certain range, so, perhaps, everything a number is negatively exceeded a buy order is placed. The Chaikin Oscillator is best used in combination with the MACD or RSI.

(tradingview.com) Figure 168: CO Oscillator #2[clvii]

SMI ERGODIC OSCILLATOR (SMIEO)

(tradingview.com) Figure 169: SMIEO Oscillator[cviii]

The SMIEO is a little-known oscillator that plots the difference between the SMI Ergodic Indicator and the signal line as a histogram. In turn, the SMI Ergodic Indicator (SMIEI) is the same as the True Strength Index (TSI), except it includes a signal line from which crossover signals can be generated. Those crossover signals are then used to generate the SMIEO. As with most crossover strategies, a negative crossover (below centerline) is bad, and a positive crossover (above centerline) is good. So, applied to the histogram, the higher the value, the better, and the lower the value, the worse. It can be used as a confirming indicator (to determine the strength of trends) and is best used in conjunction with a leading indicator or oscillator, such as the RSI or the Stochastic Oscillator.

DETRENDED PRICE OSCILLATOR (DPO)

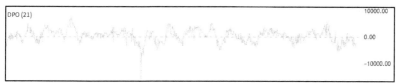

(tradingview.com) Figure 170: DPO Oscillator[clix]

The DPO is a lagging price oscillator (just like the percentage price oscillator detailed above) that attempts to remove short-term trends from price in order to analyze longer-term cyclical patterns. Cycles can be identified by counting the number of periods (for example, 1 day, 1 month, etc.) between peaks or troughs. Peaks and troughs are simply high points and low points. This information can be traded upon because, for example, you may identify that new peaks (highs) are reached roughly every three months on a given price. It would then be easy to trade upon that information. In this way, identifying general cyclical within the DPO can be very useful. It's best used in combination with other indicators.

*In this Bitcoin (BTC) chart, it can be seen that lows are hit roughly every two months, after which a quick pop resumes the overall uptrend. However, it should also be noted that the massive overall uptrend could not be predicted solely through the DPO. As the entire crypto industry settles and cyclical patterns emerge, indicators like these will become more prevalent.

(tradingview.com) Figure 171: DPO Oscillator #2[clx]

CHANDE MOMENTUM OSCILLATOR (CMO)

(tradingview.com) Figure 172: CMO Oscillator[clxi]

The Chande Momentum Oscillator (developed by Tushar Chande in 1994) uses momentum to identify price strength or lack thereof. The CMO operates within a -100 and +100 range; generally, any value over 50 is considered overbought, and values below 50 are considered oversold. Often, a 10-day or 12-day MA is added to the CMO as a signal line. Divergence is also important; a downtrending price is bullish if combined with an uptrending CMO and vice versa. The CMO should be used with confirming indicators.

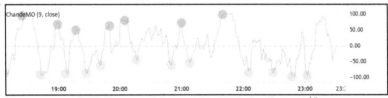

(tradingview.com) Figure 173: CMO Oscillator #2[clxii]

ULTIMATE OSCILLATOR (UO)

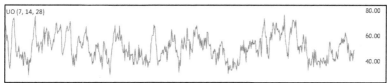

(tradingview.com) Figure 174: Ultimate Oscillator[clxiii]

The Ultimate Oscillator. created by Larry Williams in 1976, aims to measure price momentum (buying & selling pressure) across three different periods (7-day, 14-day, and 28-day). The three periods are weighted and averaged, which results in a less volatile indicator and fewer false signals (as well as fewer signals overall). The UO operates within the same rules as the RSI: limits of 0 and 100, with under 30 indicating an oversold state, and over 70 indicating an overbought state. Williams suggests several steps to confirm a buy signal; while they won't be covered at this time, they are helpful in risk management and to definitively confirm signal. If you're interested, I suggest you search "Larry Williams three steps."

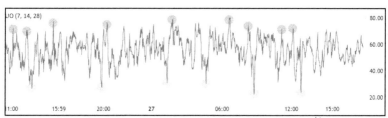

(tradingview.com) Figure 175: Ultimate Oscillator #2[clxiv]

AWESOME OSCILLATOR (AO)

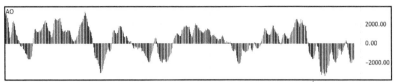

(tradingview.com) Figure 176: Awesome Oscillator[clxv]

The Awesome Oscillator is a momentum indicator created by Bill Williams (not related to Larry Williams) that aims to determine whether bulls or bears are dominating a market or asset. The AO is plotted as a histogram and can most easily be used through observing centerline (also known as zero-line) crossovers. When the oscillator value is over zero, the bears are in control and vice versa. So, buy and sell signals can be generated whenever the centerline is crossed upwards (buy) or downwards (sell). Divergence in the AO is indicative of a reversal. Given the limitations and many false signals that the AO generates, it should be used alongside various other confirming indicators.

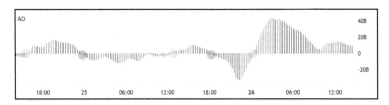

(tradingview.com) Figure 177: Awesome Oscillator #2[clxvi]

ESSENTIAL: OSCILLATORS

This Essentials section provides a recap of the top 4 most essential oscillators out of the 15 above. All are popular and provide relatively accurate signals. Please refer to the full breakdowns above concerning any of the oscillators below, and don't forget that many of the other charts on the list above do hold value; I suggest that you give all of them a try at some point in your trading career.

RSI

The RSI (Relative Strength Index) is a momentum oscillator that measures the strength or weakness of price trends and, therefore, the likeness of reversals. RSIs trade within a range of 0 to 100; a value over 70 indicates an overbought condition, and a value under 30 indicates an oversold condition.

(tradingview.com) Figure 178: RSI Oscillator #3[clxvii]

MACD

The MACD is a momentum oscillator that identifies potential trend reversals through change in momentum. The MACD operates through the MACD line (found by subtracting the 26-day EMA from the 12-day EMA), the signal line (a 6-day EMA), and a histogram, which plots divergence. Crossovers between the two lines indicate a change in momentum; a bullish crossover is the MACD passing above the signal line, and a bearish crossover is a MACD cross below the signal line. The height of the histogram is indicative of momentum strength.

(tradingview.com) Figure 179: MACD Oscillator #3[clxviii]

STOCHASTIC

The Stochastic Oscillator is a leading momentum oscillator that aims to signal potential reversals and changes in momentum before they happen. The stochastic value is plotted between 0 and 100; above 80 indicates overbought conditions and under 20 indicates oversold conditions. The Stochastic Oscillator is known to be quite accurate.

(tradingview.com) Figure 180: Stochastic Oscillator #3[clxix]

BUILDING A STRATEGY: REVISITED

This concludes the wholly-reference part of this book. In detail, hundreds of the most important patterns, indicators, concepts, and oscillators have been identified and analyzed. However, pieces must come together into a whole, and, armed with a thousand swords and subjects, you must now merge your forces into a united front. This can be done through strategy. Strategy in technical analysis involves pre-set rules, set methods (a framework), and flexibility to learn, grow, and experiment.

DEVELOP INFRASTRUCTURE

Infrastructure in investing is the software that surrounds and powers an investor. The modern game is played online; and software helps you find potential investments, evaluate those investments, and make trades. Setting up your framework begins with choosing an exchange, the most popular of which (in the US) are Coinbase, eToro, Binance US, and Kraken. The most popular global exchanges are (respectively) Binance, Coinbase Exchange, Huobi Globa, Kraken, and Bitfinex.[27] Then, you must choose a charting software. The most popular of which, and the service I recommend (not endorsed or affiliated), is TradingView, at tradingview.com. Following this, you should also check other useful software, such as sentiment analyzers (for a list of such services, check under Sentiment Analysis in the "Basic Cryptocurrency Analysis" section), calendar websites (coinmarketcal.com, etc) bot software (a full section on algorithmic trading is coming up, so hold on for that!), market data websites (onchainfx.com, coinmarketcap.com, etc), airdrop websites (airdrops.io, airdropalert.com), and bitcoinvisuals.com. With all of this software and more, you'll have the toolbox within which your tools can flourish.

---

[27] Based on current market data from coinmarketcap.com. Liable to change.

ESTABLISH RULES: ONLINE AND OFF.

Once your infrastructure is operational, the next step is to establish a set of rules that further your trading online and off. The section immediately following this, titled "investing and psychology" goes to much greater depth on the topic of rules and the reasoning behind them; but a few basic rules could look this this: set a max trade size (online rule) and stop trading after three consecutive wins or losses (offline rule).

CHOOSE CHARTS, PATTERNS, AND INDICATORS

Once infrastructure and rules are chosen and established, the competition of the strategic trifecta requires the mastery (or at least a comfortable knowledge) of the down-in-the-dirt tools that inform your technical trading decisions. This first involves a chart (candlestick, bar, Heiken-Ashi, Renko, etc.) followed by patterns (triangles, cup-and-handles, etc.) and indicators & oscillators (RSI, MFI, MACD, Bollinger Bands, Fib Arcs, MA's, etc.).

In combination, you'll now have a developed structure to capture and assemble data and make trades, tools to figure out what those trades should be, and rules to maximize the effectiveness of such trades. Of course, no good strategy can be set is stone; it must react and adjust based on new experiences and information, and you must pursue calculated and rational change among all three areas of strategy.

Strategy is basically just optimizing your experience in an environment before entering it; it's having a plan, using tools available to you, and working to improve such plans and tools based on a changing environment. If you can do that, you're better off that most; and the disciplined pursuit of excellence, in any field as much as trading, will inevitability lead to long-term success

INVESTING AND PYSCHOLOGY

Money is a very emotional experience. Money holds such sway over our lives, not to mention the world, and our relationship to money determines how we spend the most valuable currency of all; our time. 70% of married couples argue about money, 73% of Americans rank money as their number-one stress in life, and the average person spends one third of their life working for money.[28] Statistics aside, consider your personal relationship with money.[29] Money dictates how you spend your time and the things you can do, where you live, how you live, and so on. Most people judge others (judge implies negativity, it could better be said as "form opinions about" for better or worse), to some extent, on their relationship to money, and you likely compare yourself to others in regard to money all the time. While none of this is how things should be, it is how things are.

Since money holds such importance to us, the loss or gain of money, for most, is a very emotional experience. Harvard researchers found that making good trades in the market affects the brain in the same way as cocaine.[30] If you've been there, you can believe it! Beyond a base degree of natural emotions, money-related decisions are usually driven by family history, insecurity, fear, or greed, all accompanied by some degree of rationality. So, you should understand two things: psychology affects how *you* trade, and psychology affects how other people, and hence *the entire market*, moves. Bull markets and uptrends are based on greed, euphoria, optimism, and trust.[clxx] Bear markets and downtrends are based on anxiety, denial, fear, and panic. Beware of both sides of this: as we'll elaborate upon in the crypto trading rules section, nothing lasts forever, and

---

[28] 1 - Money Magazine – 2014 Survey of Couples and Money
     2 - CreditWise 2021 Survey
[29] "What Percentage of Your Life Will You Spend at Work ...."
    https://revisesociology.com/2016/08/16/percentage-life-work/.
[30] (n.d.). Functional Imaging of Neural Responses to Expectancy ... - CiteSeerX.
    https://citeseerx.ist.psu.edu/viewdoc/download?doi=10.1.1.387.7974&rep=rep1&type=pdf

thinking as rationally as possible in times of up and down is the best thing you can do. Here are a few things you can do to aid in rational thinking during emotional experiences:

WHEN TO STOP TRADING

Stop trading after three consecutive wins or losses. This can be a painful rule, albeit an effective one. If you have three consecutive good trades, you're likely to be on an emotional high. If you have three losing trades in a row, your day is officially ruined (not really, but it does suck). Either way, you are in an emotional state of mind and your ability to think rationally and make good decisions is impaired. So, at the very least, take a long break. The best thing to do is simply stop trading and resume the next day. Of course, as with all these rules, please adjust it to fit your personality; if you're an experienced and profitable Stoic, you might move to 4. If you're just starting out or know yourself to be prone to emotional trading, move it down to 2.

HAVE A MANTRA

Having a few choice words to repeat to yourself can be a quick way to reach a confident and focused state of mind. While it is much better for you to choose something that's truly meaningful to you (as the kids says, "hits different"), I'll list a few options for inspiration:

- "I am calm, focused, and confident."
- "I am confident and able."
- "Where's my money?"[31]
- "Slow and steady wins the race."
- "Brick by brick."
- "Look at me now, mom." (not really)

---

[31] Grant Cardone. If you know, you know.

TAKE BREAKS

Take breaks. Take a walk, exercise, meditate, listen to music, or get some food. In some way (preferably out of the home), relax and unwind your mind.

ESTABLISH RULES

This, if anything, is the one habit I hope to impart to you from reading this list. Most of the other tips on this list are rules that should fit within your overall rule-based strategy.

TRADE SIZE

Don't increase or decrease the size of money you're putting into a position because "you're feeling it." Adjust positions based on risk; nothing else. So, as a rule, it is best not to constantly change the amount of money you're putting into trades; if you do, it better be because of a very good analysis. Have a conversation with yourself and ask why you're making the trade you're making. What's it founded on?

TRADING JOURNAL

Many traders keep a log of all trades; they'll write down entry and exit prices, the asset, and any notes. This isn't just an activity that benefits your trading; it is also fun and can provide useful perspective.

BIASES

Every trader has unconscious biases that influence decisions. If you think you're not subject to biases, you'd then be subject to the blind-spot bias. When it comes to understanding biases, awareness is everything because biases inherently alter awareness and skew perception away from the truth. So, I hope you won't fall victim to the blind-spot bias and will instead consider yourself and your own habits from an absolute viewpoint. I don't say this to be negative (and I can't say I haven't been a hypocrite with this) but rather to make you lots of money. If you want to do that and be a better trader (and perhaps an improved person, although I'm sure you're already spectacular!), go into these biases with a magnifying glass placed directly overhead.[32]

Definitions:

A *bias* is a prejudice against or for something.

A *fallacy* is a mistaken belief.

A *heuristic* technique is an approach to problem-solving that shortcuts to an incomplete solution.

INTUITION

If you're feeling a trade, should you do it? "Feeling it" comes from intuition, and intuition is derived from patterns that you notice unconsciously (subconsciously). So, an experienced, long-time day trader might have intuition based on patterns not consciously noticed. This, ultimately, is where I'll end the question of intuition. The more experienced you are, the better your intuition will become, given our definition. When you're starting out, "I'm feeling it" will probably lead to a big, red loss. Of course, the logical question is then asking when you draw the line, is it one year, three years, or so on? My view on this is that you should take steps to test your intuition while mitigating as much risk as possible. So, perhaps trade with 1/10th of your normal volume, or perhaps don't trade but see

---

[32] Note: I recommend the book *You are Now Less Dumb* by David McRaney.

if you would have been right and adjust from there. Just make sure to recognize intuition as intuition and not greed or fear in disguise, and don't use intuition as an excuse for a bad decision. And no matter how much you're feeling it, stick to your trading plan.

SUNK COST FALLACY

The sunk cost fallacy is the tendency to continue an action or endeavor because time, money, and effort have already been sunk into it (a "sunk" cost is a cost that cannot be recovered), regardless of whether the current or eventual costs will outweigh the benefit. This fallacy is exceedingly common; hanging onto expensive clothes you don't wear, painting a room in a color you realize you don't like but continuing regardless, investing money into a business that seems to be failing, or purchasing a ticket to an event that switches locations and requires severe inconveniences to attend. In the market, if you've lost money, this fallacy makes you likely to go at it again to try and make your money back, even if the odds aren't in your favor. Beware of unconsciously making decisions because of the sunk cost fallacy.

SOCIAL PROOF

While social proof isn't a bias, it should hold a place on this list because it can impact investors profoundly, as exemplified through "hype" coins or tokens. Social proof raises perceived value and alters the perceived risk versus reward dynamic. While social proof does carry very real gains along with it and trend trading is quite literally based upon social proof and projects that "everyone's talking about," it should be taken into account that hype coins and tokens may not carry real, long-term utility and therefore may be perfect for a quick flip or short-term hold, but nothing more. At the end of the day, just do your research, don't get caught up in the hype, and identify social sentiment (since "hype" is really just an extremely positive and widespread sentiment) as a variable to be considered in all investment decisions.

AVAILABILITY BIAS

The availability bias (or availability heuristic) distorts risk perception by relying on information that first comes to mind. One may then overestimate the importance of that data and skew decision-making as per that available information. For example, someone who saw a car crash on Monday is extremely likely to make conservative driving decisions for the next few days or weeks. Despite that, the risk of driving before and after Monday hadn't changed; instead, all that changed is the availability of information about the dangers of driving. Within trading, this concept goes as follows: investment decisions can be skewed by the most available information, even if that information is not the most accurate. So, next time you're making an investment decision, take some time to consider whether the information you're trading upon takes the full puzzle into account, not just one piece. This bias also goes by the name of the overweighted familiarity bias, availability heuristic, recency bias, and frequency illusion bias.

MARTINGALE BIAS

This bias is interesting since the "martingale strategy" actually has a 100% chance of being profitable if one has enough money. Martingale strategies are so effective, given enough money, that casinos effectively banned them through the introduction of minimums and maximums. However, unfortunately, this doesn't work in trading, and the Martingale bias is something not to do, not something to do. Essentially, the strategy relies on "doubling down" on a losing investment. For example, say you have a 1% chance of winning a casino game. You'll lose 99/100 times, but, assuming you double your investment every single time, it is a mathematical certainty that you will eventually win and make back everything you lost and more because you're always putting in double what you previously put in. The Martingale strategy has since expanded to refer to putting more money in an losing investment, with the hope that the investment rises in value and the purchases farther down the line make up for the loss of the initial buy-in. So, with that being said, the Martingale bias in our context refers to the heuristic of putting more and more money in falling investments. Sometimes, this can be good, assuming that the price will recover; you'd then simply have bought the dip. However, it is a slippery slope, and there must come a point where you may want to put more money in a downed investment, but you, rationally speaking, shouldn't. Either way, I suggest that you make the decision of whether to invest in a deeply wounded coin or token with the Martingale bias in mind; this will give you the best chance of putting emotion to the side and dealing with the problem as it is—a game of probability.

HOT-HAND BIAS

The hot-hand bias is a cognitive fallacy in which a person who consecutively experiences a successful or unsuccessful outcome believes that such outcome is more likely to happen again. For example, an NBA shooter may have sunk several shots in a row. He now considers himself "on fire" and believes that he is more likely than not to make subsequent shots. Within examples such as that in which variables can be controlled, the hot-hand fallacy may not actually be a fallacy (due to the placebo effect, among other factors), but it very much is within the context of trading. So, whether you've had a string of wins or losses, you absolutely do not have a better chance of the given outcome continuing just because of the previous outcomes. I suggest above that one should stop trading after three consecutive winning trades or three consecutive losing trades in part due to this bias.

ANCHORING BIAS

Anchoring is the bias by which initial information affects the judgment of all subsequent information. For example, in a negotiation, say for an acquisition worth $50 million, the offering party might come right out the gate with an offer of $30 million. The sellers feel that they're worth $50 million, but whether they are or aren't, the entire rest of the negotiation is based on the number "$30 million." Marketers use the anchoring bias all the time to affect the perception of a product or service, and it holds even more importance in the art of negotiation (check out the book *Never Split the Difference* by Chris Voss if you're interested in learning more). While learning about a coin, token, or project for the first time, you're likely to develop an anchor. You may read an article about how bad the coin is before you look into it, or form opinions about it just by the name and price. In those ways and many more, you form a subconscious anchor that affects all subsequent decisions. Keep this in mind during initial impressions and remember that sticking to a strategy (for example, trading upon certain metrics), in large part, renders the anchoring bias a non-issue.

CONFIRMATION BIAS

The confirmation bias is an inclination to find, interpret, and recall information in a way that supports or confirms prior beliefs. Basically, people are biased towards confirming that what they already believe is correct. Confirmation bias is the reason for many arguments, erroneous situations, and flawed decisions. This bias is used against us; within social media networks, algorithms provide content that serves our prior beliefs and hence mostly restricts perception to one viewpoint. This, in part, is why people are so polarized in the US on many issues; they're literally being force-fed one, and only one, perspective. Within trading, the confirmation bias affects research, which affects perception {of companies}, which affects trading decisions. For example, you may love the juice shots of company X. When you research the company, you find that the business isn't actually doing so well, but to support your previous beliefs, you only search and read information about the positives of the business, while downplaying or making excuses for the negatives. In this way, emotional connection downplays rationality. Make sure to keep this in mind while researching investments and attempt to disregard prior beliefs as much as possible. This is especially important in technical analysis, where trades are based only on real data, and it is easy to see what you want to see in charts.

CONSERVATISM BIAS

The conservatism bias is the bias towards revising prior beliefs insufficiently when given new data. As an example, let's resume with the juice shots of Company X. You still really do love the juice, but you manage to overcome the confirmation bias and look at the hard facts, which are that the company is overspending and is badly managed. Instead of moving from the belief that *this company is great* to *this company sucks as an investment*, the conversation bias would lead you towards *"this company is fine, they'll do better one day."* In this, instead of uprooting prior beliefs in favor of a directly contrasting belief, you change your position only slightly. Basically, you're conservative in changing your ideas. You may make excuses or only focus on the most positive data. So, if you're ever looking into a coin or token that you have preconceived notions about, whether for better or worse, recognize that, and do your best to find objective data and make objective decisions.

OUTCOME BIAS

Outcome biases occurs when decisions are based on previous outcomes without considering previous processes. This one is especially brutal in trading. For example, say you hear about a friend who made a 5,000% return on Dogecoin. You may then immediately invest in Dogecoin, not because you paid attention to how or why that 50x profit happened and whether the circumstances have presented themselves again, but because your friend made a crazy amount of money and you really, really want to also make a crazy amount of money. So, judge information based on the process that created it, not solely because of the outcome, and don't get burned by "trust me, bro" tips.

ENDOWMENT EFFECT BIAS

This involves placing too much value on assets already owned and overweighting such assets relative to investments not owned. This can also consist of only trading in the industry you work in or the country you live in, despite the benefits of diversifying across multiple industries and global markets.

FRAMING BIAS

Framing biases compare relative data, as opposed to studying absolute data. For example, studying 10 bad companies will make one decent company look amazing, even if it is not actually that good in terms of absolute metrics.

LOSS AVERSION BIAS

An aversion to loss, even if not losing, results in more loss. For example, cutting losses versus holding. This doesn't necessarily mean that you should cut losses; it just means that you consider your research and understand that sometimes selling at a loss is necessary.

TRADING WITH PSYCHOLOGY IN MIND

This brings us to the end of the most important biases and fallacies that affect trading. I'll bet right now that, at some point, you'll do something described above, remember it, and hopefully make a better investment decision or general decision as a result. Even better, I hope that I've made clear the fickleness of the subconscious and imparted that establishing a strong strategy, cultivating self-awareness, and learning from experience are the best ways to combat fallacies, biases, and heuristics in trading. If you do this, you won't be fighting against yourself but rather be a collective, focused, and able force.

ALGORITHMIC TRADING

Algorithmic trading is the art of getting a computer to make money for you. Or, at least, that's the goal. Algo traders, as the slang goes, attempt to identify a set of rules that, if used as a foundation to trade upon, turn a profit. When these rules are chosen and triggered, the code will execute an order. For example, say you love trading with exponential moving average crossovers (EMAs). Whenever you see Bitcoin's 12-day EMA pass the 50-day EMA, you invest 0.01 Bitcoin. Then, you typically sell when you've made a 5% profit or, if it isn't working out, you cut your losses at 5%. It would be very easy to convert this preferred trading strategy into algorithmic trading rules. You'd code an algorithm that would track all the Bitcoin data, invest your 0.01 Bitcoin during your preferred EMA crossover, and then sell at either a 5% profit or a 5% loss. This algorithm would run for you while you sleep, while you eat, literally 24/7, or during any timeframe you wish. Since it only trades exactly as you set it, you're comfortable with the risk. Even if the algorithm works just 51 out of every 100 trades, you are turning a profit and could simply continue forever without putting in any time. Or you could consult more data and improve your algorithm to work 55 per 100 times or 70 per 100 times. Ten years later, you're now a multi-trillionaire making money every second of every day while you sip tropical juice on a sunny beach.

Sadly, it's not that easy, but that is the concept of algorithmic trading. The really nice hypothetical aspect of trading with a machine is that the income ceiling is practically limitless (or, at the very least, immensely scalable). Consider the chart on the next page. This is a visualization of an algorithm that trades 200 times per day if certain conditions are met. As in the above example, the algorithm will exit the position either at a 5% profit or a 5% loss. Let's assume that you give the algorithm $10,000 to work with, and 100% of the portfolio is put into each trade. Red signifies an unprofitable trade (a 5% loss), and green signifies a good trade, a 5% gain.

Figure 181: Algorithmic Trading Imagery[clxxi]

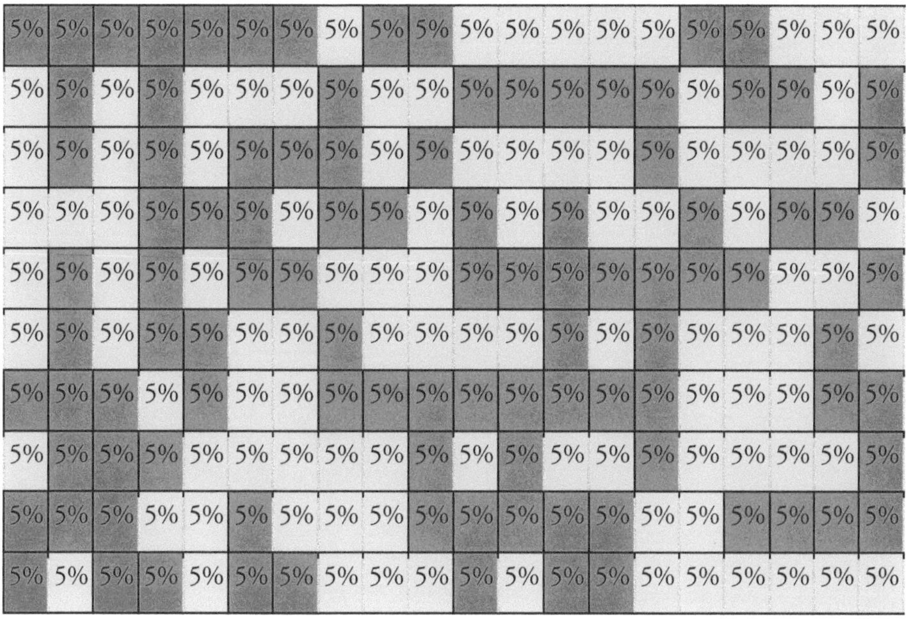

As per the chart, this algorithm is correct just 51% of the time. At this tiny majority, a $10,000 investment would become $11,025[33] in just one day, $186,791.86 in 30 days, and, after one full year of trading with your $10,000, the result would be $29,389,237,672,608,055,000. That's 29 quintillion dollars, which is roughly 783 times as much as the total value of every single US dollar in the world. Obviously, that wouldn't work. However, let's now assume that given the same rules, the algorithm makes a profitable trade just 50.1% of the time, which means 1 extra profitable trade out of every 1,000. After 1 year, this algorithm would turn $10,000 into $14,400. After 10 years, just under $400,000, and after 50 years, $835,437,561,881.32. That's 835 billion dollars.[34] This seems pretty easy. Just use historical data to test algorithms until you've found one that's at least 50.1% profitable, get $10k, and your kids will be

---

[33] Not just $11,000 because, remember, the 5% profit is compounded into the next trade. $10,000 at 5% is a $500 profit, but then $10,500 at 5% profit is $11,025.
[34] Check these numbers out for yourself with Money Chimp's compound interest calculator: http://www.moneychimp.com/calculator/compound_interest_calculator.htm

trillionaires. Sadly, this doesn't always work out, and here are some of the challenges facing algorithmic traders:

ALGORITHMIC TRADING CHALLENGES

#1: ERRORS

The most obvious challenge is that of an error-free algorithm. Many services today make the process much easier and don't require as much coding experience. However, some still require some level of coding ability and the rest a degree of technical knowledge. As I'm sure you can imagine, any misstep in creating an algorithm can result in a game-over.[35] That's why you probably shouldn't code it yourself unless you actually know how to code, in which case you should probably still consult a coder friend!

#2: UNPREDICTABLE DATA

Just as with technical analysis as a whole, the expectation that historical patterns are likely to repeat is the foundation on which algorithmic trading rests. Black-swan events[36] and unpredictable factors, such as news, global crises, quarterly reports, and so on, all can throw an algorithm off and render a previous strategy unprofitable.

#3: LACK OF ADAPTABILITY

The challenge of unpredictable data is coupled with an inability to adapt to circumstances given new, contextual data. In this way, manual updates may be required. The solution to this problem is AI that learns, improves, and tests, but this is far from reality and, if it worked, probably wouldn't be all that good for the market since a few influential players could simply monetize it for their own

---

[35] Or, as would be a nice movie plot, an algorithm randomly turns out to be perfect and ends up earning all the money in the market, resulting in a depression and a global economic collapse!

[36] Black-swan events are any random or unknown factors coming into effect.

use (given that it would be a literal money-printing machine) or share it with everyone, in which case the self-destruction challenge (below) applies.

#4: SLIPPAGE, VOLATILITY, AND FLASH CRASHES

Since algorithms play by set rules, they can be "tricked" through volatility and rendered unprofitable through slippage. For example, a small altcoin may jump several percent, whether up or down, in seconds. An algorithm might see the price hit the limit sell order and trigger liquidation, despite the price simply jumping back up to the previous price or higher.

#5: SELF-DESTRUCTION

In the hypothetical occurrence of an intelligent AI that can sort through all available data, identifies the best possible trading algorithms, put them into practice, and adapt to circumstances, multiple such AIs would eradicate their own trading strategies. For example, say 1 million of these AIs exist (really, many more people than this would use it if it became available for purchase). All of the AIs would immediately discover the best algorithm and start trading on it. If this happened, the resulting influx of volume would render the strategy useless. The same scenario does occur today, except without the AI. Really good trading strategies are likely to be discovered by multiple people, then used and shared until they no longer are profitable or as profitable as they once were. In this way, the best strategies and algorithms impede their own progress.

So, those are the challenges that prevent algorithmic trading from being the perfect, 4-hour workweek, tropical vacation-inducing, money-printing machine. That said, algorithms can certainly make money. Many large firms and companies base their business solely on profitable trading algorithms. So, while trading bots shouldn't be considered easy money, they should be regarded as a discipline to work on, as with any other business or interest. Here are some highlights of algorithmic trading and information on how you can get started:

BACKTESTING

Since algorithms take a certain input and react accordingly, algo traders can backtest algorithms against historical data. For example, going with the previous examples, if Trader X wants to make an algorithm that trades upon EMA crossovers, Trader X could test the algorithm by running it through every single year that the entire market has been in existence. The returns would then be plotted, and through split-testing, Trader X can come up with a formula that has been historically proven to work without ever actually having put money on the table. In this way, you can test your own algorithms and play around with different variables to see how they affect overall returns. To experiment with creating and using a trading algorithm, check out the websites on the next page.

Statistics			
	All trades	Long trades	Short trades
Initial capital	200000.00	200000.00	200000.00
Ending capital	212995.00	187455.00	225540.00
Net Profit	12995.00	-12545.00	25540.00
Net Profit %	6.50 %	-6.27 %	12.77 %
Exposure %	42.99 %	20.29 %	22.70 %
Net Risk Adjusted Return %	15.11 %	-30.92 %	56.25 %
Annual Return %	120.85 %	-55.75 %	353.86 %
Risk Adjusted Return %	281.12 %	-274.81 %	1558.61 %
Total transaction costs	2400.00	1200.00	1200.00
All trades	12	6 (50.00 %)	6 (50.00 %)
Avg. Profit/Loss	1082.92	-2090.83	4256.67
Avg. Profit/Loss %	0.13 %	-0.25 %	0.50 %
Avg. Bars Held	117.67	113.00	122.33
Winners	8 (66.67 %)	4 (33.33 %)	4 (33.33 %)
Total Profit	49820.00	9520.00	40300.00
Avg. Profit	6227.50	2380.00	10075.00
Avg. Profit %	0.73 %	0.28 %	1.17 %
Avg. Bars Held	145.50	128.00	163.00
Max. Consecutive	3	3	4

37 clxxii

Figure 182: Backtesting Sheet

ALGORITHMIC TRADING RESOURCES

Trality - trality.com | No code, free backtesting.

Quant Connect - quantconnect.com | Great community.

SuperAlgos - superalgos.org | Open-source platform.

Napbots - https://napbots.com/ | No coding required.

Gunbot - gunbot.shop | Very customizable.

Shrimpy - shrimpy.io | Automated social trading.

CryptoHopper - cryptohopper.com | Provides education, good UI.

CryptoHero - cryptohero.ai | Automated, easy-to-run bots.

Wunderbit - trading.wunderbit.co/en | Copy other users.

Bitsgap - bitsgap.com | All-in-one platform, including bots.

3Commas - 3commas.io | A bit advanced, nice UI.

Pionex - pionex.com | Free trading bots.

Haasonline - haasonline.com | Use bots or build your own.

Hummingbot - hummingbot.io | Offers pre-built templates.

RISK CONTROL

Backtesting is a great way to mitigate risk. The best alternative is through use of stop-losses and trailing stop-losses. Both of these tools are elaborated upon in the risk management section.

SIMPLICITY

Many people have concepts of algorithm trading that necessitate complex, multi-layered code that involves multiple, if not a dozen or more, indicators, patterns, and oscillators. Most (public) successful algorithms used by professionals and non-professionals alike are surprisingly un-complex. Most involve one indicator, or perhaps the combination of two. I suggest you follow this established route, but that said, if you do happen to discover an extremely complex and superior algorithm, I will be the first to sign up!

HIGH-FREQUENCY TRADING

It wouldn't be right to write (no pun intended) about algorithmic trading and fail to mention HFT, so I will take a moment to do it now. You've probably heard of high-frequency trading used in the stock market; it has a reputation as being bad for the little guys. However, it is very common, and the same HFT strategies proven to be profitable in the stock market are being transferred into the crypto market.

High-frequency trading is algorithmic trading on steroids. HFT utilizes computer programs to process an extreme number of orders, perhaps thousands, in fractions of seconds. High-frequency traders use volume to profit on very small differences in price. They might make a penny per transaction, but multiply that by millions of transactions, and you've got a pretty good profit.

HFT accounts for 50% of all stock trading volume in the US. That means that half of all stock trades are never even looked at by humans but rather executed by a computer in some warehouse. While HFT hasn't yet been rolled out to this extent to crypto markets, it is definitely something to look out for as a trend in the near future, or, arguably, something to take advantage of while the opportunity remains relatively unsaturated.

CRYPTO TAXES

As the saying goes, we can't avoid taxes, and such an idea certainly applies to cryptocurrency (and especially short-term trading) despite the seemingly anonymous and unregulated nature of the industry. I suggest you visit the website of your tax-collection organization to learn more about cryptocurrency taxes in your country. That said, the following information places a spotlight on US-set rules.

- In 2014, the IRS declared that virtual currencies are property, not currency.

- If cryptocurrencies are received as payment for goods or services, the fair market value (in USD) must be taxed as income.

- If you hold a coin or token for more than a year, it's classified as long-term gain, and if you bought and sold it within a year, it's a short-term gain. Short-term gains are subject to higher taxes than long-term gains.

- Income from mining virtual currencies is regarded as self-employment income (assuming the given individual is not an employee) and is subject to self-employment tax as per the fair equivalent value of the digital currencies in USD. Up to $3,000 of losses may be recognized.

- When digital currencies are sold, profits or losses are subject to capital gains tax (since the digital currencies are regarded as property) just as if a stock was sold.

CRYPTO TRADING RULES

These 5 rules, I'm glad to say, will save you both a lot of money and emotional stability. As follows:

- ◆ Nothing lasts forever

- ◆ No woulda, shoulda, coulda

- ◆ Don't be emotional

- ◆ Diversify

- ◆ Prices don't matter

NOTHING LASTS FOREVER

As of this writing, in early 2021, the crypto market is in a bubble. I say this as a crypto optimist, perhaps even a maximalist. The incredible returns people are making, and the incredible uptrends of practically all coins are simply unsustainable. If this keeps up forever, you don't need technical analysis. In fact, you wouldn't need any method of analysis. You'd just put money in anything large and make a massive profit. This doesn't mean that the market is going to zero or that the concepts that drive growth will fail; I'm simply making the case that, at some point, the tremendous growth will slow. This may be slow and gradual, or fast, as with a rapid crash. Historically, Bitcoin has operated through cycles involving massive bull runs, the largest of which occurred in late 2017, March to July of 2019, and again from November of 2020 to the time of this writing, April 2021. In the mentioned bull runs, respectively, Bitcoin went up roughly 15x (2017), 3x (2019), and now, in the current bull run, 10x and counting. In the previous case in which Bitcoin went up more than 15x, the better part of the following year was then spent crashing from 20k to 4k. This supports the idea of the mentioned Bitcoin cycles, which begin with a massive uptrend, and then end with a crash to higher lows. This means several things: one, it is a good bet to hold if Bitcoin is crashing. Two, if Bitcoin and the crypto market are going up while you're reading this, it will probably go down at some point in the next few years. If it is going down while you're reading this, it will likely go up in a truly massive way in the next few years. Of course, the market ecosystem is liable to change, but this is the exact point I want to make. Assuming that crypto reaches mass adoption and becomes an integral part of all aspects of money, business, and general life, *it will have to stabilize* at some point. That point may be in 2021, 2023, or 2030. It will likely crash and rise multiple times before steadying into a somewhat less volatile market, at least relative to its former self. When that time comes, I will update this section. I may also write an update every time the market crashes.

In doing this, I want to ingrain the idea that nothing lasts forever. I suggest doing some research and understanding the cyclical nature of Bitcoin and the crypto market. Doing so will help you keep a level head in whatever situation and direction the market might be in. These next four rules will also help very much.

Anyway, that's that, and next time you're losing a ton of money and staring down a long, dark tunnel of red, think of this.

May 2021 update: Bitcoin and the entire market has crashed, which only serves to prove the point described above.

NO WOULDA, SHOULDA, COULDA

This rule is taken from a popular and legendary stock trader and host of the show *Mad Money*, Jim Cramer. The idea is represented through no woulda, no shoulda, and no coulda. So, if you make a bad trade, take a few minutes to think about how you can learn from it and improve. Then, after that few minutes, don't think about what you *would* have done, what you *should* have done, or what you *could* have done. This will allow you to learn and improve while simultaneously keeping yourself sane. Because, at the end of the day, you always could have done it better. Don't beat yourself up about losses, and don't let wins get to your head.

DON'T BE EMOTIONAL

Emotion is the antithesis of technical trading. Technical trading predicts current and future action on historical data, and, sadly, the market doesn't care how you feel. Emotion, more often than not ("not" simply due to the random occurrence of making a good decision through a bad process), will only hurt you and take away from the trading strategies you developed. Some people are naturally comfortable with the risk and emotional rollercoaster of trading; if you're not, it's best to adjust your investment strategy to fit the personality. While all that may seem a bit over the top, just wait until you enter a massive position into a risky position and have to go to sleep, or, worst of all, sell right before a four-day, 300% pump. RIP.

DIVERSIFY

Diversification counters risk. And, as we know, crypto is risky. While you both assume and are likely looking for a certain level of risk (due to the risk-return tradeoff principle) by investing in crypto, you do (probably) have a certain level of risk that you're not comfortable with. Diversification helps you stay within that maximum load of risk. While I can't speak to your unique situation, I would recommend that any crypto investor keep a somewhat diversified portfolio, no matter how much you believe in a project. Fund allocation should (usually) be split between Bitcoin, Ethereum or ETH alternatives (such as Cardano, BNB, etc.) and various altcoins, along with some cash. While exact percentages vary depending on individual situation (35/25/30/10, 60/25/10/5, 20/20/40/20, etc.), most professionals would agree that this is the most sustainable way to invest, capture gains across the market, and lower the chance of losing a large percentage of your portfolio due to one or a few mistaken decisions (I have indeed done this). However, all that said, the crypto market isn't like other markets out there. Some traders only invest in one or two top-50 cryptos and put most of their money into small-cap altcoins. At the end of the day, establish a strategy that fits your situation, resources, and personality, and then diversify within the boundaries of that strategy.

PRICES DON'T MATTER

Given that supply and initial price can both be set, the price itself is largely irrelevant without context. Just because Binance Coin (BNB) is at $500 and Ripple (XRP) is at $1.80 doesn't mean that XRP is worth 277x the value of BNB. In fact, the two coins are currently within 10% of each other's market cap. When a cryptocurrency is first created, the supply is set by the team behind the asset. The team may choose to create 1 trillion coins, or 10 million. So, looking back at XRP and BNB, we can see that Ripple has roughly 45 billion coins in circulation, and Binance Coin has 150 million. In this way, price doesn't really matter. A coin at $0.0003 can be worth more than a coin at $10,000 in terms of market cap, circulating supply, volume, users, utility, etc. Price matters even less due to the advent of fractional shares, which lets investors invest any amount of money in a coin or token regardless of price. So, while price is still half of the market cap equation (price per unit x number of units = market cap), the second half of the equation can be rigged from the start. Many other metrics are much more important and should be considered before price. Although, I'll quickly mention, price can have a psychological impact, as has been discussed in the market psychology section.

ACKNOWLEDGEMENTS

As I write this, it's yet another late night, but one unique in being the final night. This is it; it's been the biggest book project of my life so far (out of quite a few prior) and an amazing team has been invaluable in turning this vision to a reality. I'm grateful for each of them and their priceless contributions.

Thanks to Jack Jacobs for introducing me to cryptocurrency. I'm indebted to Blake Martin, without whom I wouldn't have the same clarity, and to Cole Morgan and Henry Lin for unwavering support throughout the process and beyond, and further so to Ana Joldes, my editor, to BL, WL, and Augusto Andres for editing and formatting (not to mention style, tone, and generally everything writing) clarification and assistance. A massive thank to you to the people behind the partner blog to this book, School of Coin, and the continuing project of Textafy and SA publishing. Lastly, thanks to Ori Sherman, Hallie C, and NK. You're all awesome!

To an exciting future,

Jon Law & Alan John

RESOURCES

RESOURCES

The following section contains reference information and lists to further your exploration of cryptocurrencies and investing. This is a look at the contents of the following section:

- Essential Dictionary
- Trading Dictionary
- Exchanges
- YouTube Channels
- Podcasts
- News Outlets
- Charting Services

CRYPTO ESSENTIAL DICTIONARY

A small dictionary (glossary, if you may) is included in this book to provide a solid foundation of knowledge (if needed), a source to refer to, and full comprehension of any topics previously discussed in this book. It is split into two sections: essential terms and trading terms. Essential terms are a few handpicked, important words that must be known in order to operate with confidence in the crypto space. It is brief, but worth spending a few minutes looking through. The second section, titled "crypto trading dictionary," consists of important terms related to technical analysis, all other forms of crypto analysis, and trading as a whole. It can be used if any words previously used in this book aren't understood or covered or to build a ground-up vocabulary. If any words were missed, not understood, or otherwise should be included, please contact me at the email at the end (or start) of this book, and I'll include your suggested edits in the next edition.

ACCOUNT

An account is a pair of public and private keys (see below) from which you can control your funds. You typically view your account through an exchange, which provides an ideal trading interface (UI). However, your funds are actually stored on the blockchain, not in your account.

ADDRESS(ES)

An address, also known as your public key, is a unique collection of numbers and letters that function as an identification code comparable to a bank account number or an email address. With it, you can carry out transactions on the blockchain. Addresses have round, colorful "logos" that are called address identicons (or, simply, "icons"). These icons allow you to quickly see whether or not you input a correct address.

AIRDROP

An airdrop is a marketing tool used by new coins. The team behind a new coin or token will give users the ability to receive the asset for free, typically in exchange for a small task, such as following the company on social media or providing your email address. Airdrops are great for the project since many new customers get excited about the coin and want to see it rise in value. It is also great for users since they get the coin for free and can potentially make a lot of money. However, airdrop scams are common, and many new coins fail, so make sure to do your research to understand what new airdrops are good and what airdrops aren't. Here are a few sites that provide information about new airdrops:

- ◆ aidrops.io
- ◆ airdropalert.com
- ◆ icomarks.com
- ◆ cocoricos.io

ALGORITHM

An algorithm is the mathematical rules (the structure) that a code or software must follow. Many forms of algorithms are used across the internet, such as those used by social media services to decide which content gets how much exposure. Blockchains and cryptocurrencies use algorithms to perform a variety of tasks.

ALTCOIN(S)

Bitcoin was the first cryptocurrency, as well as the coin that popularized the industry. As a result, Bitcoin belongs to its own category, while all other coins are referred to as altcoins.

BITCOIN

Bitcoin was the first cryptocurrency. It was created in 2008 by an individual (or, more likely, a group of individuals) operating under the name Satoshi Nakamoto.

CASH

In the world of crypto and investments, cash does not mean keeping literal cash, but rather money that is not invested and is instead being held in an account as a digital balance.

CONFIRMED

This refers to a transaction being confirmed, which means multiple peers in the network have validated it. Once a transaction has been confirmed, it is permanently put in the public ledger.

DAPP(S)/DAOS

dApp is short for "decentralized application." Basically, any app that runs on a blockchain (or any other peer-to-peer network) and does not have a centralized owner is considered a dApp. DAO is shorthand for decentralized autonomous organizations and refers to any organization run by a computer and not humans.

DECRYPTION/ENCRYPTION

Encryption is the process of converting plain text into coded information through the use of a cipher. The opposite is decryption, which converts coded information into plain text. Decryption is the opposite of "encrypting." Decryption in crypto involves turning encrypted data back into plain text.

DIGITAL COMMODITY

A digital commodity is a digital asset that holds value. Digital commodities do not have to be digital currencies. They can be NFTs, digital art, or digital commodities.

DIGITAL CURRENCY

Digital currencies lie within the realm of digital commodities. Instead of referring to all digital assets, digital currencies refer to all currencies that operate only online and do not have a physical form.

DIGITAL SIGNATURE

Your digital signature is used to confirm online documents. This isn't an actual signature; instead, it refers to a code generated by an algorithm.

DISTRIBUTED LEDGER

A distributed ledger is a ledger that is stored in many different locations so that multiple parties can validate transactions. Blockchain networks use distributed ledgers.

DOLPHIN/WHALES

Crypto holders are classified through several different animals. Those with extremely large holdings, such as in the millions, are called whales, while those with moderately sized holdings are called dolphins.

DUMP

To dump, or dumping, refers to selling a large amount of cryptocurrency or a large amount of a coin or token being sold. For example, you might say, "that coin is dumping," or "I'm dumping this coin."

ERC-20/ERC-20 STANDARD

An ERC-20 is one of the many Ethereum tokens. Remember, a token is a token because it is built upon another blockchain. ERC-20 is significant in the world of Ethereum tokens because it is used to define the rules by which all tokens on the Ethereum blockchain function and creates a standardized structure. It can be likened to a security guard; it requires and ensures that all tokens in its vicinity follow that set of rules. The ERC-20 "standard" is the combined list of all the rules. Tokens using the ERC-20 standard can transact between each other and exchanges in an easier and better manner.

ETHER

Ether is the native cryptocurrency of the Ethereum blockchain. Its ticker symbol is ETH, and by using any currency on the Ethereum blockchain, you must pay the fees in Ether.

EXCHANGE

A [crypto] exchange is a marketplace where cryptocurrencies and tokens can be bought, sold, and traded. Exchanges must be combined with wallets. In wallets, coins can be held through addresses. Exchanges act as an easy intermediary to help users interact with each other.

FIAT

Fiat refers to legal and centralized government currency, such as the US dollar or Euros.

FINTECH

Fintech is short for financial technology. Fintech consists of any technology that supports and/or enables financial services. Cryptocurrencies are examples of fintech, as well as companies such as GoFundMe and PayPal.

FORK/HARD FORK/SOFT FORK

A fork is the occurrence of a new blockchain being created from another blockchain. For example, Bitcoin Cash once forked off from Bitcoin. Forks (the process is actually much more complicated than this, but here is a simple overview) occur when algorithms have a disagreement and split into two different versions. Two kinds of forks exist: a hard fork and a soft fork. A hard fork in a blockchain is a fork that occurs when all the nodes in the network upgrade to a newer version of the blockchain and leave the old version behind; two paths are then created: the new version and the old version. A soft fork contrasts this by rendering the old network invalid; this results in just one blockchain, not the two that come as a result of a hard fork.

FUNDAMENTAL ANALYSIS

Fundamental analysis is the analysis of a coin or token through its underlying value. It aims to identify the "real value" (also known as the "fair market" value) of an asset through fundamental metrics, such as revenue, profit, cash flow, and an abundance of ratios.

GAS

Gas refers to the fee required to complete transactions on the Ethereum blockchain. Gas is basically the reward given to the miners that validate and complete the transaction.

GWEI

Gwei is the denomination (the price-per-unit) used in defining the cost of Ethereum gas (see below). You can think of Gwei and Ethereum as the dollar and the penny. 1 ETH equals one billion Gwei. Gwei is used instead of Ethereum because it is somewhat easier to say that gas fees are 1 Gwei than 0.0000000001 Ether.

HALVING

Halving is the process by which the reward for mining Bitcoin is cut in half. Bitcoin halving happens every 210,000 blocks, which roughly equates to every 4 years. Halving will happen until the maximum supply (see below) of Bitcoin has been reached, and all 21 million coins have been put into circulation.

HASH/HASH RATE

A hash is a function that converts one value into another; a hash in the crypto world converts an input of letters and numbers (a string) into an encrypted output of a fixed size. Basically, hashes help with encryption. "Solving" each hash requires working backward to solve an extremely complex mathematical problem. The measure by which a computer is judged in terms of its ability to hash is called a hash rate. Put simply, the hash rate is the speed at which a node can perform hashing.

HOT WALLET/COLD WALLET

A hot wallet refers to a cryptocurrency wallet connected to the internet; the opposite, cold storage, refers to a wallet that is not connected to the internet. Hot wallets allow the account owner to send and receive tokens; however, cold storage is more secure than hot storage.

INITIAL COIN OFFERING (ICO)

To raise funds and awareness, the creators of a cryptocurrency will put an initial portion of their coins up for purchase.

INITIAL EXCHANGE OFFERING (IEO)

IEOs are similar to ICOs (initial coin offerings) In the sense that both are initial offerings of coins or tokens used solely within the crypto space. IEOs are coming into fashion as the "next ICOs" because IEOs allow online crypto trading platforms to make the asset tradeable directly. Basically, IEO's require less effort to invest in and streamline the trading process of an initial offering.

KEYS

A key is a random string of characters that are used by algorithms to encrypt data. Two keys are used for cryptocurrency: a public key and a private key. Both are important to understand and defined below in depth.

MINING

Mining is the process by which blocks are added to a blockchain by solving a mathematical problem. Solving these problems takes an extremely large amount of computational power; hence, rewards are provided to those who do the work. People or organizations who use their computational power to mine are known as "miners."

NETWORK

A network, at its core, is an interconnected system. The system within a cryptocurrency network is made up of many nodes that assist the blockchain in various tasks. Basically, a crypto network can be thought of as many different computers working together to run the blockchain.

NODE

A node is a computer (a node can be any computer; there aren't any special types) connected to a blockchain's network and assists the blockchain in writing and validating blocks. Some nodes download an entire history of their blockchain; these are called master nodes (see below for full definition) and perform more tasks than regular nodes. Additionally, nodes are not tied to a specific network; nodes can switch to different blockchains practically at will, as is the case with mining multipool mining (see below).

PEER-TO-PEER (P2P)/P2P NETWORKS

A peer-to-peer network involves many computers working with each other to complete tasks. Peer-to-peer networks do not require a central authority and are an integral part of blockchain networks.

PRIVATE KEY/PUBLIC KEY

Cryptocurrency users will utilize two keys: a public key and a private key. Both keys are strings of letters and numbers. Once a user initiates their first transaction, a pair of public and private keys is created. The public key is used to receive cryptocurrencies, while the private key allows the user to carry out transactions from their account. Both keys are stored in a crypto wallet.

PROTOCOL(S)

A protocol is a system or procedure that controls how something should be done. Within cryptocurrency, it is a governing layer of code. For example, a security protocol determines how security should be carried out, a blockchain protocol governs how blockchain acts and operates, and a Bitcoin protocol controls how Bitcoin functions.

PUMP/DUMP

A pump is a rapid upward price movement in a coin or token. A dump is a rapid downward price movement in a coin or token. "To the moon" refers to a massive pump or someone hoping for a massive pump.

RANK/RANKING

Cryptocurrencies are ranked by market cap; within the ranking system (you can think of it as a scoreboard), being in the top 10 is a kind of badge of honor. You'll often hear people say, "I think that coin can be in the top 10," and similar statements. Bitcoin has held the top spot pretty much indefinitely and likely will hold that top spot for the foreseeable future. Check out the coin rankings for yourself at any of the following sites or at any others you may know of:

- ♦ cryptoslate.com
- ♦ coingecko.com
- ♦ coinmarketcap.com

SATOSHI NAKAMOTO

Satoshi Nakamoto is the individual, or possibly the group of individuals who created Bitcoin. Not much is known about this mysterious figure, and his anonymity has spawned countless conspiracy theories. While Nakamoto lists himself as a 45-year-old male from Japan on an official peer-to-peer foundations website, he uses British idioms in his emails. Additionally, the timestamps of his work (fun fact: Nakamoto coded a secret message into the first mined block of Bitcoin) aligns better with someone based in the US or the UK. Most believe that his disappearance was planned (many have connected his work to biblical references), and others believe a governmental organization, such as the CIA, was linked to his disappearance. You should keep in mind that these are nothing more than fringe theories; however, what remains a fact is that the creator of Bitcoin currently holds a fortune worth more than $50 billion (Nakamoto owns 1.1

million Bitcoins), and if Bitcoin goes up another few hundred percent, this anonymous billionaire, the father of cryptocurrency, will be the richest person in the world.

SEED/SEED PHRASE

A seed phrase is interchangeable with a mnemonic phrase (see below). Seed phrases are 12-to-24-word sequences that identify and represent a wallet. With it, you can never lose access to your account. If you forget it, there's no way to reset it or get it back. Anyone who has your seed phrase has full access to your wallet and cryptocurrency holdings.

SMART CONTRACT(S)

Smart contracts are an essential part of the cryptocurrency world. A smart contract is a self-executing contract that is run on code. The terms of the contract and the execution are directly written into the smart contract by the code, and, therefore, this removes the issue of trust for all parties in the transaction. Transactions issued with smart contracts are irreversible and untraceable. These contracts can be used not just for managing cryptocurrency transactions but also for government voting systems, various other financial services, information storage, and many other industries.

STABLECOIN

A stablecoin, similar to a pegged currency, is a coin or token that is designed to remain at the same price as a designated asset, typically a bank-issued currency. For example, USDT and DAI are two popular stablecoins that are pegged to the US dollar. So, 1 USDT is designed to always equal 1 US dollar. Stablecoins have very low volatility, typically earn a few percent interest (APY) per year, and are generally a good place to store crypto holdings.

TECHNICAL ANALYSIS

Technical analysis is a type of analysis that looks at technical indicators to predict price movement. Technical analysts use historical data from charts to make their predictions.

TICKER/TICKER SYMBOL

A ticker is a sequence of letters that identifies a specific coin or token. All stocks, as well as cryptocurrencies, have these ticker symbols. For example, Bitcoin is BTC and Ethereum is ETH.

TOKEN(S)

A cryptocurrency token is a kind of digital currency that represents an asset, just like coins. However, while coins are built upon their own blockchain, tokens are built upon another blockchain. Many tokens use the Ethereum blockchain and are thus referred to as tokens, not coins. Coins are used only as money, while tokens can have a wider range of uses. Token uses are represented under subcategories, the most essential of which are security tokens, platform tokens, utility tokens, and governance tokens. Understanding tokens is an integral part of understanding what exactly you're trading, as well as understanding all uses of digital currencies, and for those reasons, we will take a look at the token types just mentioned.

- Security tokens represent legal ownership of an asset, whether digital or physical. The word "security" in security tokens doesn't mean security as in being safe, but rather, "security" refers to any financial instrument that holds value and can be traded. Basically, security tokens represent an investment or asset.

- Utility tokens are built into an existing protocol and can access the services of that protocol. Remember, protocols provide rules and a structure for nodes to follow, and utility tokens can be used for wider purposes than just as payment tokens. For example, utility tokens are commonly given to investors during an ICO. Then, later on, investors can use the utility tokens they received to pay on the platform they received the tokens from. The major thing to keep in mind is that utility tokens can do more than just serve as a means to buy or sell goods and services.

♦ Governance tokens are used to create and run a voting system for cryptocurrencies that allows system upgrades without a centralized owner.

♦ Payment (transactional) tokens are used solely to pay for goods and services.

TRANSACTION

A transaction is any exchange between multiple parties. A cryptocurrency transaction involves one party buying a coin or token and another party selling that coin or token. Thousands of cryptocurrency transactions are completed per second.

UNPERMISSIONED LEDGER(S)

Unpermissioned ledgers are ledgers that have no single owner. The purpose of such a ledger is to allow for all the benefits of decentralization.

WALLET(S)

A wallet is the UI (the user interface, refer to definition) used to manage your account(s). For example, Coinbase and Exodus are common wallets.

CRYPTO TRADING DICTIONARY

BEAR FLAG/BULL FLAG

A bear flag is an indication on a coin or token chart that a downtrend is likely. A bull flag is the opposite of a bear flag.

BEAR TRAP/BULL TRAP

A bear trap refers to false signals on a chart that signal a downtrend is likely. This is referred to as a "trap" because traders who take a bear trap as an indication of a downtrend may short the coin or token, hence losing money when the price actually increases. A bull trap is the opposite of a bear trap.

BEAR (BEARISH)/BULL/BULLISH

To be a bear means that you think the price of a coin, token, or the value of the market as a whole is going to go down. If you think like this, you're also considered "bearish" on the given security. The opposite is to be bullish. A person who thinks a security will rise in value is bullish on that security.

BUBBLE

A bubble in crypto and all investments refers to when everything is going up, usually at an unsustainable rate. Often, bubbles will pop and trigger a large crash. For this reason, being in a bubble, whether referring to the market as a whole or a specific coin or token, is both a good and a bad thing.

BUY WALL

A buy wall occurs when a large limit order (see below for definition) is placed to buy a cryptocurrency at a given value. This "buy wall" can prevent the asset from falling below that value since demand at that price will be greater than supply.

CONFLUENCE/CONFLUENCE TRADING

Confluence occurs when you combine multiple strategies and indicators into one strategy. Confluence trading is an extension of this; it refers to a trader who utilized confluence in their trading strategy.

CORRECTION

A correction is a price movement downward after a quick jump or a peak in price. For example, a move from $10 to $25 may result in a correction to $20, where support is then found.

DEAD CAT BOUNCE

A dead cat bounce is a term that refers to a brief recovery in price before a large crash.

DEPTH CHART

A depth chart graphs requests to buy or sell a coin or token. The depth chart displays a crossover point in which transactions are quickly completed (typically if a market order is placed) and at what price people are willing to buy and sell the coin or token.

DUMP

To dump, or dumping, refers to selling a large amount of cryptocurrency or to a large amount of a coin or token being sold. For example, "that coin is dumping," or "I'm dumping this coin."

FILL OR KILL ORDER (FOK)

A fill or kill order is an order that must be executed upon immediately. If this doesn't happen, the trade will be canceled. FOKs are used to ensure that a large position is completed in a very short period of time.

FUNDAMENTAL ANALYSIS

Fundamental analysis is the analysis of a coin or token through its fundamental metrics.

GOLDEN CROSS

A golden cross is a chart pattern that involves a short-term moving average (for example, a 10-day MA) crossing above a long-term moving average (Perhaps a 50-day MA).

LEVERAGE

Traders can "leverage" their money by taking on debt. For example, say you have $1,000, and you're using 5x leverage; you're now trading with $5,000 worth of funds. By that same function, 10x leverage would be $10,000, and 100x would be $100,000. Like margin trading (see below), leverage allows you to amplify profits by using money that isn't yours and keeping the extra profit. However, leverage trading is very risky; generally speaking, leverage trading is not recommended unless you're an experienced trader and have some financial stability.

LIMIT ORDER/BUY/SELL

When you mean to execute a trade, you may choose to have that trade executed in several different manners. One of such manners is through a market order (see full definition), which means that you choose to have your order executed immediately at the best price available. Another alternative is a limit order; this allows you to choose the price at which you buy or sell a coin or token. For example, say a coin is trading at $240. If you choose to buy 1 coin with a market order, that order will immediately execute, perhaps at $240, or perhaps at $239 or $241. If you place a limit order, you choose what price you'd like to buy the coin at. Maybe this coin is volatile, so you decide to place a limit buy order at

$237 in the hopes that the price will spike down to your level at some point throughout the day and then recover and continue in an uptrend. In that case, the order would only execute when the coin's price hits $237 or below. Generally, limit orders are good for such situations—catching the price slightly below what it is at. (That said, to be clear, you can set a limit order for any price). If you don't really care whether your purchase point is 2% lower or not (or whatever it may be), you can just set a market order and purchase the security instantly.

LONG/SHORT [POSITION]

Taking a long position means that the trader intends to hold that security for the long term; this generally means at least a few months. A short position is the opposite; the trader intends to get in and get out in a relatively short time period, whether minutes, hours, or days.

MARGIN TRADING

Margin trading is a popular strategy whereby traders borrow funds, called "on margin," to place trades. For example, someone with $10,000 may trade with a 5x margin, which gives them access to $50,000 of capital. Then, if the trade works out, they repay the $50,000 and keep the extra profit. Margin trading is very risky and should only be performed by experienced investors because if trades go bad, margin traders may owe more than they have. Basically, the rewards are massive, but the risks are just as so.

MARKET CAPITALIZATION (MARKET CAP)

The market cap of a coin is the total trading value. This can easily be calculated by multiplying the total supply of a coin by the coin's price. For example, a coin at $5 with a supply of 1 million units has a market cap of $5 million. Bitcoin's market cap is well past half a trillion dollars.

MARKET MOMENTUM

The momentum of a market is the ability of that market to maintain periods of growth or downfall. For example, a market that has been going up for 6 months has momentum, while the same can be said if that market plunges into bear territory and stays there.

MARKET ORDER

A market order is one of several types of orders that can be placed when you mean to execute a trade. Market orders are immediately filled at the best price available. The opposite, limit orders, allows the buyer to choose the price they want their trade to be fulfilled at. While market orders may result in the purchase point being slightly higher, they allow for quicker entry.

OVERSOLD/OVERBOUGHT

An oversold cryptocurrency has had much more selling pressure than buying pressure; as a result, it has been sold to a price that is considered below its fundamental value. Therefore, being oversold generally means that the security should rebound at least to its fundamental (true) value. Overbought is the opposite; this occurs when a coin or token has been brought up to what may be considered an unjustifiably high price. Generally, if someone believes that a coin or token is oversold, they predict that it will go up (at least in the short term, and to what extent may certainly differ), and if they believe it is overbought, they predict that it will go up.

PUMP

A pump is a rapid upward price movement in a coin or token.

PUMP AND DUMP

A pump and dump is a scheme carried out by a trader or, more typically, a group of traders. In a pump and dump, the starting group will buy a large amount of a coin or token. Other investors think that the price will continue to go higher and also buy in. Then, once the price has been significantly inflated, the original investors dump their shares and take their profit. This practice is looked down upon since it causes a lot of unknowing investors to lose money.

RESISTANCE

Resistance in technical analysis is a price that an asset finds difficult to break through since many people find that a good price to sell at. Sometimes, levels of resistance can be physiological. For example, Bitcoin might hit resistance at $50,000, since many people were thinking, "when Bitcoin hits $50,000, I will sell." Often, when a resistance level is broken through, the price can quickly climb. For example, if Bitcoin did break past $50,000, it might quickly climb to $55,000, at which time it may face more resistance. Support is the opposite of resistance.

SELL WALL

A sell wall is a very large sell order at a limit price. Sell walls drive prices downwards. The opposite is a buy wall, which can stop a coin or token from falling beneath a certain price, in which sellers have to sell a massive amount of the asset in order to complete the limit buy order and drive the price farther downwards.

SLIPPAGE

Slippage can occur when a trade is placed with a market order. Remember, market orders try to execute at the best possible price. (See below for full definition.) Sometimes, a notable difference between the expected price and the actual price occurs. For example, you may want to buy 10 Examplecoin for $1000. You place a market order; however, you end up only getting 9 Examplecoin for your $1000. Slippage can occur for several reasons (if you're interested, definitely check out some outside sources), but all you really need to know and what slippage is and how it can affect you. If you're placing a large order, you may want to place a limit order (see below) as opposed to a market order. This will eliminate all danger of slippage.

SUPPORT

A price of a coin or token at which that asset is less likely to fall through since many people are willing to buy the asset at that price and therefore there is much "support." Often, if a coin hits support levels, it will reverse into an uptrend. This may be a good time to buy. Although its support levels are broken through, the coin is likely to fall further to another support level.

SWING/SWING TRADERS

A swing is a dramatic reversal and movement in price. Swing traders try to catch and trade upon market and specific crypto swings.

TANK/TANKED

Refers to an asset taking a massive dive, e.g., "it tanked from $20 to $10."

TECHNICAL ANALYSIS

Technical analysis is a type of analysis that looks at technical indicators to predict price movement. Technical analysts use historical data from charts to make their predictions.

VOLATILITY

Volatility is the ability and likelihood of a coin or token to change rapidly, whether up or down. For example, a coin that moves 10% up one day, 27% down the next day, and 40% the day after that is more volatile than a coin that moves up 2%, down 0.5%, and up another 1%. Some coins, called stablecoins (see below), have very little volatility, while some coins or tokens, typically those with a relatively small market cap, are extremely volatile and move up and down rapidly.

WICKS/WHISKERS/SHADOWS

Wicks are the lines extending from the colored bars on candlestick charts. Whiskers refer to the low-high range of the given asset.

EXCHANGES

- Binance - binance.com (binance.us for US residents)
- Coinbase – coinbase.com
- Kraken – kraken.com
- Crypto – crypto.com
- Gemini – gemini.com
- eToro – etoro.com

YOUTUBE CHANNELS

- Hasoshi

  https://www.youtube.com/c/Hashoshi4

- Digital Asset News

  https://www.youtube.com/c/DigitalAssetNewsDAN

- Benjamin Cowen

  https://www.youtube.com/channel/UCRvqjQPSeaWn-uEx-w0XOIg

- Coin Bureau

  https://www.youtube.com/c/CoinBureau

- DappUniversity

  https://www.youtube.com/c/DappUniversity

- Forflies

  https://www.youtube.com/c/Forflies

- DataDash

  https://www.youtube.com/c/DataDash

- The Crypto Lark

  https://www.youtube.com/c/TheCryptoLark

- Crypto Jebb -

  https://www.youtube.com/channel/UCviqt5aaucA1jP3qFmorZLQ

- Sheldon Evans

  https://www.youtube.com/c/SheldonEvansx

- BitBoy Crypto

  https://www.youtube.com/channel/UCjemQfjaXAzA-95RKoy9n_g

- Real-Crypto

  https://www.youtube.com/channel/UC93MJYEjwCW3-9ipq09k7XQ

- Colin Talks Crypto

  https://www.youtube.com/channel/UCnqJ2HjWhm7MbhgFHLUENfQ

- MDX Crypto

  https://www.youtube.com/user/Beanfield123

- Crypto Insight

  https://www.youtube.com/channel/UCl2metIgoJpgBAFiKBDmVEA

- The House of Crypto

  https://www.youtube.com/channel/UCojKnjrW3D5wT81MMm8l4EA

- Crypto Mike

  https://www.youtube.com/channel/UCAOEOYGEhQNVT1ZNqp42e3g

- Ivan on Tech

  https://www.youtube.com/user/LiljeqvistIvan/videos

- Suppoman

  https://www.youtube.com/user/Suppoman2011/videos

- Crypt0

  https://www.youtube.com/user/obham001/videos

- Anthony Pompliano
  https://www.youtube.com/channel/UCevXpeL8cNyAnww-NqJ4m2w

- Aimstone
  https://www.youtube.com/channel/UC7S9sRXUBrtF0nKTvLY3fwg/about

- Chico Crypto
  https://www.youtube.com/channel/UCHop-jpf-huVT1IYw79ymPw

- Crypto Love
  https://www.youtube.com/channel/UCu7Sre5A1NMV8J3s2FhluCw/featured

- Lark Davis
  https://www.youtube.com/channel/UCl2oCaw8hdR_kbqyqd2klIA/about

- Boxmining
  https://www.youtube.com/channel/UCxODjeUwZHk3p-7TU-IsDOA

- DataDash
  https://www.youtube.com/channel/UCCatR7nWbYrkVXdxXb4cGXw/videos

- Altcoin Daily https://www.youtube.com/channel/UCbLhGKVY-bJPcawebgtNfbw

PODCASTS

- What Bitcoin Did by Peter McCormack (Bitcoin)

- Untold Stories (early stories)

- Unchained by Laura Shin (interviews)

- Baselayer by David Nage (discussions)

- The Breakdown by Nathaniel Whittemore (short)

- Crypto Campfire Podcast (relaxed)

- Ivan on Tech (updates)

- HASHR8 by Whit Gibbs (technical)

- Unqualified Opinions by Ryan Selkis (interviews)

- Crypto 101 (education)

NEWS OUTLETS

- CoinDesk – coindesk.com

- CoinTelegraph – cointelegraph.com

- TodayOnChain – todayonchain.com

- NewsBTC – newsbtc.com

- Bitcoin Magazine – bitcoinmagazine.com

- Crypto Slate – cryptoslate.com

- Bitcoin.com – news.bitcoin.com

- Blockonomi – blockonomi

- The Block – theblockcrypto.com

- Bitcoinist – bitcoinist.com

CHARTING SERVICES

- TradingView – tradingview.com

- CryptoView – cryptoview.com

- Altrady – Altrady.com

- Coinigy – Coinigry.com

- Coin Trader - CoinTrader.Pro

- CrytpoWatch – CryptoWat.ch

ALGORITHMIC TRADING RESOURCES

Trality - trality.com | No code, free backtesting.

Quant Connect - quantconnect.com | Great community.

SuperAlgos - superalgos.org | Open-source platform.

Napbots - https://napbots.com/ | No coding required.

Gunbot - gunbot.shop | Very customizable.

Shrimpy - shrimpy.io | Automated social trading.

CryptoHopper - cryptohopper.com | Provides education, good UI.

CryptoHero - cryptohero.ai | Automated, easy-to-run bots.

Wunderbit - trading.wunderbit.co/en | Copy other users.

Bitsgap - bitsgap.com | All-in-one platform, including bots.

3Commas - 3commas.io | A bit advanced, nice UI.

Pionex - pionex.com | Free trading bots.

Haasonline - haasonline.com | Use bots or build your own.

Hummingbot - hummingbot.io | Offers pre-built templates.

BOOKS

Before continuing on to crypto books, I'm going to take a moment to shamelessly plug another book I wrote called *The Modern Guide to Stock Market Investing for Teens: How to Ensure a Life of Financial Freedom Through the Power of Investing*. The book was rated as the #1 book for youth to learn about investing by Investopedia, and thousands of buyers (not to mention 100+ 4.4 star reviewers on Amazon) have used it to introduce young people across the world to the superpower of investing. I'd love to give you a free audiobook version of the book, and if you'd like it please email me at alanjohnpublishing@gmail.com. Only the first 20 people to reach out will can get the free code. The book is available for sale at most major online book sellers. Thanks!

- *Mastering Bitcoin* – Andreas M. Antonopoulos
- *The Internet of Money* - Andreas M. Antonopoulos
- *The Bitcoin Standard* – Saifedean Ammous
- *The Age of Cryptocurrency* – Paul Vigna
- *Digital Gold* – Nathaniel Popper
- *Bitcoin Billionaies* – Ben Mezrich
- *The Basics of Bitcoins and Blockchains* – Antony Lewis
- *Blockchain Revolution* – Don Tapscott
- *Cryptoassets* - Chris Burniske and Jack Tatar
- *The Age of Cryptocurrency* - Paul Vigna and Michael J. Casey

INDEX

BIBLIOGRAPHY

1. (39), matle85, et al. "Crypto Valuation: How Important Is Circulating Supply?" *Steemit*, steemit.com/cryptocurrency/@matle85/crypto-valuation-how-important-is-circulating-supply.

2. "10 Best ICO White Paper Examples in Terms of Structure and Design." *AGENTE*, agentestudio.com/blog/10-best-ico-white-paper-examples-structure-and-design.

3. "The 12 Tenets of Sound Fundamental Analysis and Valuation Principles." *Old School Value*, 22 Mar. 2016, www.oldschoolvalue.com/stock-valuation/the-12-tenets-of-sound-fundamental-analysis-and-valuation-principles/.

4. "20 Best FREE Crypto Trading Bots for Binance, KuCoin [2021]." *Guru99*, www.guru99.com/best-crypto-trading-bot.html#:~:text=Crypto%20trading%20bots%20are%20a.

5. "2019 Blockchain Year in Review: The Top 7 Trends We Saw." *Skalex.io*, 7 May 2020, www.skalex.io/2019-blockchain-year-in-review/#defi.

6. "3 Things Everyone Should Know About the Availability Heuristic." *Farnam Street*, 6 June 2020, fs.blog/2011/08/mental-model-availability-bias/.

7. "3 Trading Indicators to Combine with the Klinger Oscillator." *Tradingsim*, 8 Aug. 2018, tradingsim.com/blog/klinger-oscillator/.

8. "The 3 Types of White Papers (& When to Use Them)." *Compose.ly*, 29 Sept. 2020, compose.ly/strategy/types-of-white-papers/.

9. 3599. "Top Crypto Trends for 2021 Every Trader Should Know: Finance Magnates." *Finance Magnates | Financial and Business News*, Finance Magnates, 9 Feb. 2021, www.financemagnates.com/thought-leadership/top-crypto-trends-for-2021-every-trader-should-know/.

10. "The 7 Best Price Action Patterns Ranked by Reliability." *Samurai Trading Academy*, 3 Nov. 2019, samuraitradingacademy.com/7-best-price-action-patterns/#:~:text=1B.&text=The%20head%20and%20shoulders%20patterns,(the%20head)%20between%20them.

11. "70 Cryptocurrency Youtube Channels To Follow in 2021." *Feedspot Blog*, 6 May 2021, blog.feedspot.com/cryptocurrency_youtube_channels/.

12. "83 Candlestick Pattern Indicators for TradeStation." *TechnicalTradingIndicators.com*, www.technicaltradingindicators.com/tradestation-indicators/83-candlestick-patterns/.

13. "Accumulation Distribution (ADL)." *TradingView*, www.tradingview.com/support/solutions/43000501770-accumulation-distribution-adl/#:~:text=Definition.

14. ADALove, and Krishna. "Is Cardano Deflationary?" *Cardano Forum*, 19 Feb. 2018, forum.cardano.org/t/is-cardano-deflationary/8438.

15. "Algorithmic Trading - Hard Facts." *ClickAlgo*, clickalgo.com/algorithmic-trading-hardfacts#:~:text=Professional%20traders%20do%20not%20have,once%20these%20conditions%20are%20identified%2C.

16. "Algorithmic Trading." *IG*, www.ig.com/en/trading-platforms/algorithmic-trading.

17. Aloosh, Arash, and Samuel Ouzan. "The Psychology of Cryptocurrency Prices." *Finance Research Letters*, Elsevier, 16 May 2019, www.sciencedirect.com/science/article/pii/S1544612318309036.

18. altFINS. "Trading Moving Averages - Part 1 (Using EMA 12/50 Crossovers)." *AltFINS*, 11 Dec. 2020, altfins.com/trading-moving-averages-part-1-using-ema-12-50-crossovers.

19.   Alton, Larry. "Why the Fibonacci Sequence Is Your Key to Stock Market Success." *The BiggerPockets Blog | Real Estate Investing & Personal Finance Advice*, 17 Jan. 2018, www.biggerpockets.com/blog/fibonacci-sequence.

20.   "Altrady - Fastest Trading Platform." *Altrady Crypto Trading Software Is Fast, Easy & Secure|Trade Bitcoin*, www.altrady.com/.

21.   "Analytical Charting and Trading Platform." *GoCharting*, GoCharting, gocharting.com/.

22.   "Anchoring Bias - Biases & Heuristics." *The Decision Lab*, 22 Jan. 2021, thedecisionlab.com/biases/anchoring-bias/.

23.   "Anchoring Bias - Definition, Overview and Examples." *Corporate Finance Institute*, 15 Apr. 2019, corporatefinanceinstitute.com/resources/knowledge/trading-investing/anchoring-bias/.

24.   "Andrews' Pitchfork." *Andrews' Pitchfork [ChartSchool]*, school.stockcharts.com/doku.php?id=chart_analysis%3Aandrews_pitchfork.

25.   "Are 90% of Amateur Algorithmic Traders Losing Money Just like 90% of Amateur Day Traders?" *Quora*, www.quora.com/Are-90-of-amateur-algorithmic-traders-losing-money-just-like-90-of-amateur-day-traders.

26.   "Automated Cryptocurrency Trading." *AlgoTrader*, 24 Feb. 2021, www.algotrader.com/features/automated-cryptocurrency-trading/.

27.   "Awesome Oscillator (AO) - Technical Indicators - Indicators and Signals." *TradingView*, www.tradingview.com/scripts/awesomeoscillator/.

28.   BabyPips.com. "How to Trade Triangle Chart Patterns in Forex." *BabyPips.com*, BabyPips.com, 22 Apr. 2021, www.babypips.com/learn/forex/triangles.

29.   BabyPips.com. "Schiff Pitchfork." *BabyPips.com*, BabyPips.com, 21 May 2020, www.babypips.com/forexpedia/schiff-pitchfork.

30.   Banton, Caroline. "Kicker Pattern." *Investopedia*, Investopedia, 15 Feb. 2021, www.investopedia.com/terms/k/kickerpattern.asp.

31.   Benzinga, Source: "The 5 Biggest Trends In Cryptocurrency For 2020." *CFO*, 3 Dec. 2019, www.cfo.com/payments/2019/12/the-5-biggest-trends-in-cryptocurrency-for-2020/.

32.   Berthou, Adrien. "Token Supply 101: Fundamentals of Token Supply-and Monetary Policy." *Medium*, Medium, 20 Aug. 2020, medium.com/@AdrienBe/token-supply-101-fundamentals-of-token-supply-and-monetary-policy-a20cc761f6ec.

33.   "The Best Charting Tools For Crypto Traders." *RSS*, cryptotrader.tax/blog/the-best-charting-tools-for-crypto-traders#:~:text=TradingView%20is%20by%20far%20the,free%20users%20and%20pro%20users.

34.   "Best Momentum Indicators for Day Trading." *Warrior Trading*, 9 June 2020, www.warriortrading.com/best-momentum-indicators/.

35.   "Best Strategies to Use with the Stick Sandwich Candlestick Pattern." *Tradingsim*, 30 Oct. 2020, tradingsim.com/blog/stick-sandwich/.

36.   Best, Raynor de. "Low Supply Cryptocurrency 2021." *Statista*, 12 May 2021, www.statista.com/statistics/802775/worldwide-cryptocurrency-maximum-supply/.

37.   Binance Academy. "A Guide to Cryptocurrency Fundamental Analysis." *Binance Academy*, Binance Academy, 19 Feb. 2021, academy.binance.com/en/articles/a-guide-to-cryptocurrency-fundamental-analysis.

38.   Binance Academy. "Circulating Supply." *Binance Academy*, Binance Academy, 17 Sept. 2019, academy.binance.com/en/glossary/circulating-supply.

39. Binance Academy. "Maximum Supply." *Binance Academy*, Binance Academy, 17 Sept. 2019, academy.binance.com/en/glossary/maximum-supply.

40. Birru, Justin, and Baolian Wang. "Nominal Price Illusion." *Journal of Financial Economics*, Elsevier, 1 Jan. 1970, econpapers.repec.org/article/eeejfinec/v_3a119_3ay_3a2016_3ai_3a3_3ap_3a578598.htm#:~:text=A%20zero%2Dcost%20option%20portfolio,to%20a%20lower%20nominal%20price.

41. Birru, Justin, and Baolian Wang. "Nominal Price Illusion." *Journal of Financial Economics*, North-Holland, 22 Jan. 2016, www.sciencedirect.com/science/article/abs/pii/S0304405X16000349.

42. "Bitcoin & Altcoin Trading Bot Pricing - HaasBot Plans." *HaasOnline*, 28 Oct. 2020, www.haasonline.com/pricing/.

43. "Bitcoin (BTC) Live Price Charts, Trading, and Alerts." *Cryptowatch*, cryptowat.ch/.

44. "BitMoon v1.0 for BITSTAMP:BTCUSD by Koi_Capital." *TradingView*, www.tradingview.com/chart/BTCUSD/orZhMwak-BitMoon-v1-0/.

45. Bitsgap. "Bitcoin & Cryptocurrency Trading Platform." *Bitsgap*, bitsgap.com/?ref=851dc57d.

46. Blenkinsop, Connor. "How Supply Affects Crypto's Value, Explained." *Cointelegraph*, Cointelegraph, 2 Dec. 2019, cointelegraph.com/explained/how-supply-affects-cryptos-value-explained.

47. Blocks, Ara. "Market Capitalization for Max- vs Unlimited-Supply Cryptocurrencies." *Medium*, Medium, 26 July 2018, arablocks.medium.com/market-capitalization-for-max-vs-unlimited-supply-cryptocurrencies-ceeafe008751.

48. Board, FXSSI - Forex Sentiment. "Candlestick Patterns in Forex and What Do They Mean." *FXSSI*, 6 Apr. 2021, fxssi.com/forex-candlestick-patterns.

49. Book Editor(s): Michael PompianSearch for more papers by this author, et al. "Conservatism Bias." *Wiley Online Library*, John Wiley & Sons, Ltd, 12 Sept. 2015, onlinelibrary.wiley.com/doi/10.1002/9781119202400.ch5.

50. Boutros, Michael. "Foundations of Technical Analysis: Building a Trading Strategy." *DailyFX*, 14 Oct. 2020, www.dailyfx.com/forex/education/trading_tips/daily_trading_lesson/2017/10/20/Foundations-of-Technical-Analysis-Building-a-Trading-Strategy-MB.html.

51. Bowman, Richard, et al. "Fundamental vs. Technical Analysis - Beginner's Guide with Pros & Cons." *LEHNER INVESTMENTS*, 7 Apr. 2021, catanacapital.com/blog/fundamental-vs-technical-analysis-beginners-guide/.

52. Boyte-White, Claire. "What Are the Main Differences between a Symmetrical Triangle Pattern and a Pennant?" *Investopedia*, Investopedia, 14 Jan. 2021, www.investopedia.com/ask/answers/013015/what-are-main-differences-between-symmetrical-triangle-pattern-and-pennant.asp.

53. *Brave New Coin*, bravenewcoin.com/insights/cryptocurrency-trading-bots.

54. "Build a Crypto Trading Bot | Tips and Best Practices." *DevTeam.Space*, 6 Mar. 2021, www.devteam.space/blog/how-to-build-a-crypto-trading-bot/.

55. Bulkowski, Thomas N. "Bulkowski on Candlestick Patterns." *Candlestick Patterns*, thepatternsite.com/CandleEntry.html.

56. "Bullish Kicker Candlestick Pattern." *Hit Run Candlesticks*, hitandruncandlesticks.com/bullish-kicker-candlestick-pattern/.

57. "Burned: CoinMarketCap." *RSS*, coinmarketcap.com/alexandria/glossary/burned#:~:text=Cryptocurrency%20tokens%20

or%20coins%20are%20burned%20when%20they%20are%20permanently,wallet%20
where%20they%20are%20stored.

58. "Burned: CoinMarketCap." *RSS*,
coinmarketcap.com/alexandria/glossary/burned#:~:text=Cryptocurrency%20tokens%20
or%20coins%20are%20burned%20when%20they%20are%20permanently,wallet%20
where%20they%20are%20stored.

59. Butor. "Butor/Blackbird." *GitHub*, github.com/butor/blackbird.

60. "Candlestick Pattern Dictionary." *Candlestick Pattern Dictionary [ChartSchool]*,
school.stockcharts.com/doku.php?id=chart_analysis%3Acandlestick_pattern_dictionary.

61. CaseyStubbs. "Fibonacci Retracement Channel Trading Strategy." *Trading Strategy
Guides*, Trading Strategy Guides, 29 Oct. 2020, tradingstrategyguides.com/fibonacci-
retracement-channel-trading-strategy/.

62. "Chaikin Oscillator." *Chaikin Oscillator [ChartSchool]*,
school.stockcharts.com/doku.php?id=technical_indicators%3Achaikin_oscillator#:~:text
=The%20Chaikin%20Oscillator%20is%20the,the%20momentum%20behind%20the
%20movements.

63. "Chande Momentum Oscillator (CMO)." *Trading Technologies*, 15 Oct. 2015,
www.tradingtechnologies.com/xtrader-help/x-study/technical-indicator-
definitions/chande-momentum-oscillator-cmo/.

64. "Chande Momentum Oscillator." *Fidelity*, www.fidelity.com/learning-center/trading-
investing/technical-analysis/technical-indicator-guide/cmo.

65. "Chapter 2 Candlestick Patterns." *5Paisa*, www.5paisa.com/school/candlestick-patterns.

66. Chen, James. "Algorithmic Trading Definition." *Investopedia*, Investopedia, 13 Jan.
2021,www.investopedia.com/terms/a/algorithmictrading.asp#:~:text=While%20it%20p
rovides%20advantages%2C%20such,and%20immediate%20loss%20of%20liquidity.

67. Chen, James. "Andrews' Pitchfork." *Investopedia*, Investopedia, 7 Apr. 2021,
www.investopedia.com/terms/a/andrewspitchfork.asp#:~:text=Andrews'%20Pitchfork%
20is%20a%20technical,potential%20breakout%20and%20breakdown%20levels.&text
=The%20reason%20this%20indicator%20is,is%20created%20in%20the%20chart.

68. Chen, James. "Andrews' Pitchfork." *Investopedia*, Investopedia, 7 Apr. 2021,
www.investopedia.com/terms/a/andrewspitchfork.asp.

69. Chen, James. "Chaikin Oscillator Definition." *Investopedia*, Investopedia, 27 Apr. 2021,
www.investopedia.com/terms/c/chaikinoscillator.asp.

70. Chen, James. "Chaikin Oscillator Definition." *Investopedia*, Investopedia, 27 Apr. 2021,
www.investopedia.com/terms/c/chaikinoscillator.asp.

71. Chen, James. "Doji." *Investopedia*, Investopedia, 30 Apr. 2021,
www.investopedia.com/terms/d/doji.asp.

72. Chen, James. "Double Bottom." *Investopedia*, Investopedia, 30 Apr. 2021,
www.investopedia.com/terms/d/doublebottom.asp.

73. Chen, James. "Fibonacci Fan." *Investopedia*, Investopedia, 15 Oct. 2020,
www.investopedia.com/terms/f/fibonaccifan.asp.

74. Chen, James. "Fibonacci Fan." *Investopedia*, Investopedia, 15 Oct. 2020,
www.investopedia.com/terms/f/fibonaccifan.asp.

75. Chen, James. "Hot Hand Definition." *Investopedia*, Investopedia, 12 Apr. 2021,
www.investopedia.com/terms/h/hot-hand.asp.

76. Chen, James. "Ichimoku Kinko Hyo." *Investopedia*, Investopedia, 7 Jan. 2021,
www.investopedia.com/terms/i/ichimokuchart.asp#:~:text=The%20Ichimoku%20Kink
o%20Hyo%2C%20or,span%20B%20and%20chikou%20span.

77. Chen, James. "Ichimoku Kinko Hyo." *Investopedia*, Investopedia, 7 Jan. 2021,
www.investopedia.com/terms/i/ichimokuchart.asp#:~:text=The%20Ichimoku%20Kink
o%20Hyo%2C%20or,span%20B%20and%20chikou%20span.

78. Chen, James. "Morning Star." *Investopedia*, Investopedia, 16 Sept. 2020,
www.investopedia.com/terms/m/morningstar.asp.

79. Chen, James. "Oscillator Definition." *Investopedia*, Investopedia, 29 Nov. 2020,
www.investopedia.com/terms/o/oscillator.asp#:~:text=Oscillators%20are%20momentu
m%20indicators%20used,or%20oversold%20signals%20to%20traders.

80. Chen, James. "Rising Three Methods Definition." *Investopedia*, Investopedia, 28 Aug.
2020, www.investopedia.com/terms/r/rising-three-methods.asp.

81. Chen, James. "Survivorship Bias Definition." *Investopedia*, Investopedia, 23 Nov. 2020,
www.investopedia.com/terms/s/survivorshipbias.asp#:~:text=Survivorship%20bias%20o
r%20survivor%20bias,those%20that%20have%20gone%20bust.

82. Chen, James. "Survivorship Bias Definition." *Investopedia*, Investopedia, 23 Nov. 2020,
www.investopedia.com/terms/s/survivorshipbias.asp.

83. Chen, James. "Technical Analysis of Stocks and Trends." *Investopedia*, Investopedia, 30
Apr. 2021, www.investopedia.com/terms/t/technical-analysis-of-stocks-
andtrends.asp#:~:text=The%20two%20major%20types%20of,by%20looking%20at%2
0specific%20patterns.

84. Chen, James. "Triangle Definition." *Investopedia*, Investopedia, 17 Sept. 2020,
www.investopedia.com/terms/t/triangle.asp#:~:text=A%20triangle%20is%20a%20chart
,categorize%20triangles%20as%20continuation%20patterns.

85. Chen, James. "Volume Price Trend Indicator (VPT)." *Investopedia*, Investopedia, 19
Mar. 2021, www.investopedia.com/terms/v/vptindicator.asp.

86. Chen, James. "What Is Stock Analysis?" *Investopedia*, Investopedia, 7 May 2021,
www.investopedia.com/terms/s/stock-
analysis.asp#:~:text=There%20are%20two%20basic%20types,company%20assets%2C
%20and%20market%20share.

87. Chernukha, Vasiliy. "3 Candlestick Patterns That Fail." *IQ Option Broker Official Blog*,
18 Feb. 2019, blog.iqoption.com/en/3-candlestick-patterns-that-fail/.

88. Cherry, Kendra. "How the Availability Heuristic Affects Your Decision Making."
Verywell Mind, 18 Nov. 2019, www.verywellmind.com/availability-heuristic-2794824.

89. Cherry, Kendra. "Types of Cognitive Biases That Distort How You Think." *Verywell
Mind*, 20 Jan. 2021, www.verywellmind.com/cognitive-biases-distort-thinking-
2794763.

90. Chris Douthit, Chris Douthit, and Chris Douthit. "17 Stock Chart Patterns All Traders
Should Know." *Option Strategies & Stock Market News*, 3 Apr. 2020,
optionstrategiesinsider.com/blog/17-stock-chart-patterns-to-look-for-when-analyzing-
stocks/.

91. Cointelegraph. "What Is A White Paper And How To Write It." *Cointelegraph*,
Cointelegraph, 24 Apr. 2018, cointelegraph.com/ico-101/what-is-a-white-paper-and-
how-to-write-it.

92. *Compound Interest Calculator*,
www.moneychimp.com/calculator/compound_interest_calculator.htm.

93. "Comprehensive Candlestick Patterns Guide." *Steve Nison's Candlecharts.com*, 5 Oct.
2020, candlecharts.com/candlestick-training/candlestick-patterns/.

94. Conway, Luke. "Bitcoin Halving: What You Need to Know." *Investopedia*,
Investopedia, 18 Mar. 2021, www.investopedia.com/bitcoin-halving-

4843769#:~:text=A%20Bitcoin%20halving%20event%20is,which%20new%20Bitcoin
s%20enter%20circulation.

95. "Crypto Trading Robot: Free Crypto Trading Bot." *Pionex*, www.pionex.com/en-US/.

96. "The Crypto Whitepaper Database - All Crypto Whitepapers." *The Whitepaper
     Database*, 11 Aug. 2020, www.allcryptowhitepapers.com/whitepaper-overview/.

97. "Cryptocurrencies Ranked by Volume." *CoinGecko*,
     www.coingecko.com/en/coins/high_volume.

98. "Cryptocurrencies with a Fixed Max Supply." *CryptoList*, cryptoli.st/lists/fixed-supply.

99. "Cryptocurrencies with Highest Trading Volume." *Yahoo! Finance*, Yahoo!,
     finance.yahoo.com/u/yahoo-finance/watchlists/crypto-top-volume-24hr/.

100. "Cryptocurrency Prices, Charts & Crypto Market Cap." *CoinCheckup*,
     coincheckup.com/.

101. "Cryptocurrency Prices, Charts And Market Capitalizations." *CoinMarketCap*,
     coinmarketcap.com/.

102. "Cryptocurrency Technical Analysis 101." *OKEx*,
     www.okex.com/academy/en/cryptocurrency-technical-analysis-
     101#:~:text=Though%20technical%20analysis%20in%20the,or%20decrease%20in%2
     0the%20future.

103. "CryptoFeed: A Currated Steam Of Crypto YouTube Content From Top Crypto
     Influencers." *CryptoWeekly*, cryptoweekly.co/crypto-youtube/.

104. "CryptoView: Cryptocurrency Portfolio Manager & Multi-Exchange Trading
     Platform." *CryptoView.com*, 19 Mar. 2021, www.cryptoview.com/.

105. *Currency.com*, currency.com/how-to-read-and-use-the-awesome-oscillator-trading-
     indicator#:~:text=The%20Awesome%20Oscillator%20Indicator%20.

106. Curtis, Glenn. "Trading Psychology: Why the Mind Matters in Making Money."
     Investopedia, Investopedia, 16 Sept. 2020,
     www.investopedia.com/articles/trading/02/110502.asp.

107. "Custom Award Plaques." *PlaqueMaker*,
     www.plaquemaker.com/awards?gclid=CjwKCAjwnPOEBhA0EiwA609ReUv5GvGHru
     EkL0OT1LZA7bCufFqw8aeEeE5cdU9cTXbwGWK7v6g91RoCyOsQAvD_BwE.

108. Cyborg. "How to Apply Technical Analysis to Cryptocurrencies." *SwissBorg*, SwissBorg,
     8 Feb. 2021, swissborg.com/blog/how-to-apply-technical-analysis-to-cryptocurrencies.

109. "Definition of Daily Active Addresses (DAA)." *CoinGecko*,
     www.coingecko.com/en/glossary/daily-active-addresses.

110. "The Deflationary Economics of the Bitcoin Money Supply." *Skalex.io*, 7 May 2020,
     www.skalex.io/deflationary-economics-bitcoin/.

111. *Design and Trade Algorithmic Trading Strategies in a Web Browser, with Free Financial
     Data, Cloud Backtesting and Capital - QuantConnect.com*, www.quantconnect.com/.

112. Desjardins, Jeff. "12 Types of Technical Indicators Used by Stock Traders." *Visual
     Capitalist*, 11 Mar. 2019, www.visualcapitalist.com/12-types-technical-indicators-
     stocks/.

113. "Detrended Price Oscillator (DPO)." *Detrended Price Oscillator (DPO) [ChartSchool]*,
     school.stockcharts.com/doku.php?id=technical_indicators%3Adetrended_price_osci.

114. "Detrended Price Oscillator (DPO)." *Fidelity*, www.fidelity.com/learning-
     center/trading-investing/technical-analysis/technical-indicator-guide/dpo.

115. "Doji Star Candlestick Pattern: Complete Guide." *PatternsWizard*, 30 Sept. 2020,
     patternswizard.com/doji-star-candlestick-
     pattern/#:~:text=A%20Doji%20Star%20candlestick%20pattern,current%20trend%20o

f%20the%20market.&text=Doji%20candlestick%20pattern%20is%20formed,a%20pl
us%20sign%20or%20cross.

116. Lessons on Survivorship Bias That Will Help You Make Better Decisions." *I Done This Blog*, 24 Sept. 2019, blog.idonethis.com/7-lessons-survivorship-bias-will-help-make-better-decisions/.

117. Dorman, Jeff. "Jeff Dorman: Fundamental Investing Is Alive and Well in Crypto." *CoinDesk*, CoinDesk, 5 Feb. 2021, www.coindesk.com/fundamental-investing-alive-well-crypto.

118. Downey, Lucas. "Rounding Bottom Definition." *Investopedia*, Investopedia, 7 May 2021,www.investopedia.com/terms/r/roundingbottom.asp#:~:text=A%20rounding%20bottom%20is%20a,in%20long%2Dterm%20price%20movements.

119. Elearnmarkets. "Technical Indicators: Types of Technical Indicators." *Elearnmarkets*, www.elearnmarkets.com/school/units/technical-indicators.

120. "Encyclopedia of Candlestick Charts." *Google Books*, Google, books.google.com/books?id=bgh4gAeKwCYC&newbks=1&newbks_redir=0&lpg=PP1&dq=Thomas+Bulkowski&pg=PP1#v=onepage&q&f=false.

121. "Ether Explained - Chapter 6: Ethereum vs. Bitcoin (Part 1)." *Investerest*, investerest.vontobel.com/en-se/articles/13356/ether-explained---chapter-6-ethereum-vs-bitcoin-part-1/.

122. Facebook.com/hedgewithcrypto. "4 Best Crypto Charting Software & Tools For Altcoin Traders." *Hedgewithcrypto*, 11 May 2021, www.hedgewithcrypto.com/crypto-charting-sites/.

123. Farley, Alan. "The 5 Most Powerful Candlestick Patterns." *Investopedia*, Investopedia, 7 May 2021, www.investopedia.com/articles/active-trading/092315/5-most-powerful-candlestick-patterns.asp.

124. Fernando, Jason. "Moving Average (MA) Definition." *Investopedia*, Investopedia, 29 Apr. 2021, www.investopedia.com/terms/m/movingaverage.asp.

125. Fernando, Jason. "Moving Average Convergence Divergence (MACD) Definition." *Investopedia*, Investopedia, 29 Apr. 2021, www.investopedia.com/terms/m/macd.asp.

126. Fernando, Jason. "Relative Strength Index (RSI)." *Investopedia*, Investopedia, 7 May 2021, www.investopedia.com/terms/r/rsi.asp.

127. "Fibonacci Fans." *Fibonacci Fans [ChartSchool]*, school.stockcharts.com/doku.php?id=chart_analysis%3Afibonacci_fan.

128. "Fibonacci Retracements Explained for Beginners." *Warrior Trading*, 1 June 2020, www.warriortrading.com/fibonacci-retracement-definition/.

129. *FIBONACCI SEQUENCE*, www.geom.uiuc.edu/~demo5337/s97b/fibonacci.html#:~:text=First%2C%20calculate%20the%20first%2020,F%5Bn%2D2%5D.&text=2.,F%5Bn%2D1%5D.

130. "Financial Statistics." *Money Habitudes*, www.moneyhabitudes.com/financial-statistics/.

131. "Fixed vs Unlimted Supply In Crypto And Fiat." *Nimera*, www.nimera.io/blog/crypto-fixed-vs-unlimted-supply#:~:text=In%20crypto%20ecosystems%2C%20everything%20is,is%20actually%20never%20really%20unlimited.

132. Folger, Jean. "Pros and Cons of Automated Trading Systems." *Investopedia*, Investopedia, 28 Aug. 2020, www.investopedia.com/articles/trading/11/automated-trading-systems.asp.

133. Folger, Jean. "Using Technical Indicators to Develop Trading Strategies." *Investopedia*, Investopedia, 14 Apr. 2021, www.investopedia.com/articles/trading/11/indicators-and-strategies-explained.asp.

134. "Four-Price Doji." *CandleScanner*, www.candlescanner.com/candlestick-patterns/four-price-doji/#:~:text=Four%2DPrice%20Doji%20is%20a,cases%2C%20with%20a%20single%20transaction.

135. "Free and Open-Source Crypto Trading Bots." *Superalgos*, superalgos.org/.

136. "Fundamental Analysis - Overview, Components, Top-down vs. Bottom-Up." *Corporate Finance Institute*, 2 Jan. 2020, corporatefinanceinstitute.com/resources/knowledge/trading-investing/fundamental-analysis/.

137. "Fundamental Analysis in Cryptocurrency Trading." *Gemini*, www.gemini.com/cryptopedia/fundamental-analysis-crypto-trade.

138. "Gann Square of Nine – How to Trade Using This Forecasting Tool." *Tradingsim*, 29 Jan. 2021, tradingsim.com/blog/day-trade-using-gann-square/.

139. "Gann Square of Nine – How to Trade Using This Forecasting Tool." *Tradingsim*, 29 Jan. 2021, tradingsim.com/blog/day-trade-using-gann-square/.

140. Ganti, Akhilesh. "Falling Three Methods Definition." *Investopedia*, Investopedia, 27 Apr. 2021, www.investopedia.com/terms/f/falling-three-methods.asp.

141. *Glassnode Studio - On-Chain Market Intelligence*, studio.glassnode.com/metrics?a=BTC&category=Addresses&chartStyle=column&m=addresses.ActiveCount.

142. "Glossary." *ROSALIND*, rosalind.info/glossary/fibonacci-sequence/#:~:text=The%20first%2012%20terms%20of,original%20question%20to%20his%20readers.

143. Gordon Scott, CMT. "Flag Definition." *Investopedia*, Investopedia, 24 Feb. 2021, www.investopedia.com/terms/f/flag.asp.

144. Greco, Jim. "The Difficulty of Scaling an Algo Trading Business to the Opportunity." *Medium*, Medium, 3 June 2016, medium.com/@jgreco/the-difficulty-of-scaling-your-business-to-the-opportunity-in-algo-trading-4858cd8a3f8a.

145. Guazzo, Gianmarco. "What Are the Best Books to Learn Bitcoin?" *Medium*, Coinmonks, 28 Dec. 2020, medium.com/coinmonks/what-are-the-best-books-to-learn-bitcoin-409aeb9aff4b.

146. "Gunbot - Automated Crypto Trading Bot - Buy Gunbot Here." *GunBot Shop*, gunbot.shop/.

147. Halton, Clay. "Outcome Bias Definition." *Investopedia*, Investopedia, 28 Aug. 2020, www.investopedia.com/terms/o/outcome-bias.asp.

148. Hayes, Adam. "Bollinger Band®." *Investopedia*, Investopedia, 30 Apr. 2021, www.investopedia.com/terms/b/bollingerbands.asp.

149. www.investopedia.com/terms/c/chandemomentumoscillator.asp.

150. Hayes, Adam. "Chande Momentum Oscillator Definition." *Investopedia*, Investopedia, 16 Apr. 2021, www.investopedia.com/terms/c/chandemomentumoscillator.asp.

151. Hayes, Adam. "Exponential Moving Average (EMA)." *Investopedia*, Investopedia, 29 Apr. 2021, www.investopedia.com/terms/e/ema.asp#:~:text=An%20exponential%20moving%20average%20(EMA)%20is%20a%20type%20of%20moving,the%20most%20recent%20data%20points.

152. Hayes, Adam. "Head And Shoulders Pattern." *Investopedia*, Investopedia, 29 Apr. 2021, www.investopedia.com/terms/h/head-shoulders.asp.

153. Hayes, Adam. "Inside the Risk/Reward Ratio." *Investopedia*, Investopedia, 7 May 2021, www.investopedia.com/terms/r/riskrewardratio.asp#:~:text=What%20Is%20the%20Risk%2FReward,undertake%20to%20earn%20these%20returns.

154. Hayes, Adam. "Introduction to Technical Analysis Price Patterns." *Investopedia*, Investopedia, 30 Apr. 2021, www.investopedia.com/articles/technical/112601.asp.

155. Hayes, Adam. "On-Balance Volume (OBV)." *Investopedia*, Investopedia, 7 May 2021, www.investopedia.com/terms/o/onbalancevolume.asp.

156. Hayes, Adam. "Stochastic Oscillator." *Investopedia*, Investopedia, 30 Apr. 2021, www.investopedia.com/terms/s/stochasticoscillator.asp#:~:text=A%20stochastic%20oscillator%20is%20a,moving%20average%20of%20the%20result.

157. Hayes, Adam. "Technical Analysis Definition." *Investopedia*, Investopedia, 7 May 2021, www.investopedia.com/terms/t/technicalanalysis.asp.

158. Hayes, Adam. "White Paper: What Everyone Should Know." *Investopedia*, Investopedia, 4 Mar. 2021, www.investopedia.com/terms/w/whitepaper.asp.

159. Hays, Demelza. "Why Bitcoin Is Technically an Inflationary Currency-Even Though Its Purchasing Power Is Increasing: Demelza Hays, Andrés Coronado." *FEE Freeman Article*, Foundation for Economic Education, 8 Sept. 2018, fee.org/articles/why-bitcoin-is-technically-an-inflationary-currency-even-though-its-purchasing-power-is-increasing/#:~:text=According%20to%20the%20mainstream%20economic,stabilize%20in%20the%20long%2Drun.

160. Hays, Demelza. "Why Bitcoin Is Technically an Inflationary Currency-Even Though Its Purchasing Power Is Increasing: Demelza Hays, Andrés Coronado." *FEE Freeman Article*, Foundation for Economic Education, 8 Sept. 2018, fee.org/articles/why-bitcoin-is-technically-an-inflationary-currency-even-though-its-purchasing-power-is-increasing/#:~:text=According%20to%20the%20mainstream%20economic,stabilize%20in%20the%20long%2Drun.

161. Hertig, Alyssa, et al. "Bitcoin Halving 2020, Explained." *CoinDesk*, 17 Dec. 2020, www.coindesk.com/bitcoin-halving-explainer.

162. "High Frequency Trading (HFT) Definition." *Nasdaq*, www.nasdaq.com/glossary/h/high-frequency-trading#:~:text=The%20second%20type%20of%20high,computer%2Dbacked%20high%20frequency%20trading.

163. *History and Applications - Fibonacci Numbers*, amsi.org.au/ESA_Senior_Years/SeniorTopic1/1d/1d_4history_2.html#:~:text=was%20first%20discussed%20in%20Europe,to%20many%20branches%20of%20mathematics.

164. "A History of Technical Analysis." *Winton*, www.winton.com/longer-view/reading-between-the-lines-technical-analysis-through-the-ages.

165. Holmes, Jamie. "What Are the Best Charting Platforms for Cryptocurrency Trading?" *Medium*, Coinmonks, 7 Jan. 2021, medium.com/coinmonks/what-are-the-best-charting-platforms-for-cryptocurrency-trading-85aade584d80.

166. "Home." *11 Most Essential Stock Chart Patterns | CMC Markets*, www.cmcmarkets.com/en/trading-guides/stock-chart-patterns.

167. "Home." *Day Trading*, www.daytrading.com/klinger-volume-oscillator.

168. "Home." *Day Trading*, www.daytrading.com/percent-volume-oscillator-pvo.

169. Horton, Melissa. "Is It Better to Use Fundamental Analysis, Technical Analysis, or Quantitative Analysis to Evaluate Long-Term Investments?" *Investopedia*, Investopedia, 23 Jan. 2021, www.investopedia.com/ask/answers/050515/it-better-use-fundamental-analysis-technical-analysis-or-quantitative-analysis-evaluate-longterm.asp.

170. Horton, Melissa. "Is It Better to Use Fundamental Analysis, Technical Analysis, or Quantitative Analysis to Evaluate Long-Term Investments?" *Investopedia*, Investopedia, 23 Jan. 2021, www.investopedia.com/ask/answers/050515/it-better-use-fundamental-analysis-technical-analysis-or-quantitative-analysis-evaluate-longterm.asp.

171. "How Does Risk and Reward Work in Cryptocurrency?" *Yahoo! Finance*, Yahoo!, finance.yahoo.com/news/does-risk-reward-cryptocurrency-180010707.html.

172. "How to Become A Wizard at White Papers." *Cryptocurrency Dictionary*, decryptionary.com/what-is-cryptocurrency/how-to-become-wizard-white-papers/#:~:text=A%20white%20paper%20is%20created,individuals%20for%20technic ally%20interested%20buyers.

173. "How To Control Your Emotions When Trading." *Trading Pedia*, www.tradingpedia.com/how-to-control-your-emotions-when-trading/.

174. "How To Use 'Awesome Oscillator' In Trading Strategy." *Moneycontrol*, MoneyControl, www.moneycontrol.com/news/business/markets/technical-classroom-how-to-use-awesome-oscillator-in-trading-strategy-4201371.html.

175. Hyerczyk, James. "How To Use Gann Indicators." *Investopedia*, Investopedia, 11 May 2021, www.investopedia.com/articles/trading/08/gann-indicator.asp.

176. "Ichimikichiki / Ichibot-Client-App." *GitLab*, gitlab.com/Ichimikichiki/ichibot-client-app.

177. "Ichimoku Cloud - Definition, Components, and Limitations." *Corporate Finance Institute*, 28 Mar. 2019, corporatefinanceinstitute.com/resources/knowledge/trading-investing/ichimoku-cloud/.

178. Igoe, Declan. "Crypto Trading Bots: The Ultimate Beginner's Guide." *Trality Blog*, Trality Blog, 20 Apr. 2021, www.trality.com/blog/crypto-trading-bots.

179. "Introduction to Candlesticks." *Introduction to Candlesticks [ChartSchool]*, school.stockcharts.com/doku.php?id=chart_analysis%3Aintroduction_to_candlesticks.

180. "Introduction to Point & *(tradingview.com)* Figure Charts." *Introduction to Point & (tradingview.com) Figure Charts [ChartSchool]*, school.stockcharts.com/doku.php?id=chart_analysis%3Apnf_charts%3Apnf_basics.

181. "Japanese Candlestick Charting Techniques." *Google Books*, Google, books.google.com/books?id=rbn8NeXOYV4C&newbks=1&newbks_redir=0&lpg=PP1 &dq=Steve+Nison+Japanese+Candlestick+Charting+Techniques.&pg=PP1#v=onepage &q&f=false.

182. KarlVonBahnhof. "Crypto Market Psychology vs Your Trading Psychology." *AltcoinTrading.NET*, AltcoinTrading.NET, 9 Sept. 2020, www.altcointrading.net/strategy/crypto-market-psychology/.

183. "Klinger Oscillator." *TIMETOTRADE*, wiki.timetotrade.com/Klinger_Oscillator.

184. Klumov, Gregory. "The Top 5 Trends Defining Crypto in Late 2020." *Cointelegraph*, Cointelegraph, 9 Aug. 2020, cointelegraph.com/news/the-top-5-defining-trends-for-crypto-in-late-2020.

185. Kowalski, Kyle, et al. "18 Wealth Lessons from 'The Psychology of Money' by Morgan Housel." *Sloww*, 17 Dec. 2020, www.sloww.co/psychology-of-money-book/.

186. Kuepper, Justin. "Channeling: Charting a Path to Success." *Investopedia*, Investopedia, 4 Feb. 2021, www.investopedia.com/trading/channeling-charting-path-to-success/.

187. Kuepper, Justin. "Fibonacci and the Golden Ratio: Using Technical Analysis to Unlock the Markets." *Investopedia*, Investopedia, 30 Apr. 2021, www.investopedia.com/articles/technical/04/033104.asp.

188. Kuepper, Justin. "Fibonacci and the Golden Ratio: Using Technical Analysis to Unlock the Markets." *Investopedia*, Investopedia, 30 Apr. 2021, www.investopedia.com/articles/technical/04/033104.asp.

189. Kuepper, Justin. "Pennant Definition." *Investopedia*, Investopedia, 3 Nov. 2020, www.investopedia.com/terms/p/pennant.asp.

190. Lamb, Robert. "How Are Fibonacci Numbers Expressed in Nature?" *HowStuffWorks Science*, HowStuffWorks, 30 June 2020, science.howstuffworks.com/math-concepts/fibonacci-nature.htm#:~:text=Seed%20heads%2C%20pinecones%2C%20fruits%20and,will%20be%20a%20Fibonacci%20number.

191. Landau, Elizabeth. "The Fibonacci Sequence Is Everywhere-Even the Troubled Stock Market." *Smithsonian.com*, Smithsonian Institution, 25 Mar. 2020, www.smithsonianmag.com/science-nature/fibonacci-sequence-stock-market-180974487/.

192. Leader, Mikhail GoryunovA proven. "How to Make Your Own Cryptocurrency Trading Bot: Bitcoin Algorithmic Trading Tutorial." *3Commas Cryptocurrency Blog - Trading Guides and Tutorials*, 4 Nov. 2020, 3commas.io/blog/how-to-build-your-own-crypto-trading-bot-guide#where-to-download-an-existing-open-source-bitcoin-trading-bot.

193. "Leading and Lagging Indicators: What You Need to Know." *IG*, www.ig.com/us/trading-strategies/leading-and-lagging-indicators--what-you-need-to-know-190806.

194. "Learn about Analyzing Stock Fundamentals: Debt and Equity, Techniques, and Tools." *Fidelity*, www.fidelity.com/learning-center/trading-investing/fundamental-analysis/analyzing-stock-fundamentals-learning-path.

195. Lien, Kathy. "Forex Trading the Martingale Way." *Investopedia*, Investopedia, 29 Aug. 2020, www.investopedia.com/articles/forex/06/martingale.asp.

196. Liquid. "How to Do Fundamental Analysis for Cryptocurrency." *Liquid.png*, blog.liquid.com/how-to-do-fundamental-analysis-for-cryptocurrency.

197. Liquid. "How to Trade Cryptocurrency Using Moving Averages." *Liquid.png*, blog.liquid.com/how-to-trade-cryptocurrency-using-moving-averages#:~:text=Moving%20averages%20are%20a%20popular,based%20on%20previous%20price%20action.

198. Liquid. "Understanding Cryptocurrencies with Limited Supply." *Liquid.png*, blog.liquid.com/limited-cryptocurrency-supply.

199. "List of Technical Indicators." *Trading Technologies*, 15 Oct. 2015, www.tradingtechnologies.com/xtrader-help/x-study/technical-indicator-definitions/list-of-technical-indicators/.

200. Lobel, Ben. "How to Manage the Emotions of Trading." *DailyFX*, www.dailyfx.com/education/trading-discipline/manage-the-emotions-of-trading.html.

201. Lopez, Jude. "Why This Matters: Bitcoin Active Addresses Decouple from Price." *AMBCrypto*, 8 Jan. 2021, ambcrypto.com/why-this-matters-bitcoin-active-addresses-decouple-from-price/.

202. Malone, Ryan. "White Paper Marketing: 5 White Paper Types and When to Use Them." *Inbound Marketing Agency*, www.smartbugmedia.com/blog/white-paper-marketing-5-white-paper-types-and-when-to-use-them.

203. MarketVolume.com. "PVO." *Percentage Volume Oscillator | PVO Indicator*, MarketVolume.com, 3 Nov. 2019, www.marketvolume.com/technicalanalysis/pvo.asp.

204. McFarlane, Greg. "Percentage Price Oscillator – An 'Elegant Indicator'." *Investopedia*, Investopedia, 28 Aug. 2020, www.investopedia.com/articles/investing/051214/use-percentage-price-oscillator-elegant-indicator-picking-stocks.asp.

205. McKie, Steven. "A Guide to Algorithmic Trading in Crypto." *Medium*, Amentum, 15 Apr. 2019, medium.com/amentum/algorithmic-trading-in-crypto-b0b706ffd52c.

206. Milton, Adam. "What Is a Trailing Stop Loss in Day Trading?" *The Balance*, 18 Nov. 2020, www.thebalance.com/trailing-stop-1031394#:~:text=A%20trailing%20stop%20loss%20is,the%20stop%20stays%20in%20place.

207. Milton, Adam. "What Is the Difference Between a Long Trade and a Short Trade?" *The Balance*, 1 June 2020, www.thebalance.com/long-and-short-trading-term-definitions-1031122#:~:text=1%EF%BB%BF%20A%20long%20trade,price%20and%20realize%20a%20profit.

208. Mitchell, Cory. "Commodity Channel Index (CCI) Definition and Uses." *Investopedia*, Investopedia, 10 Feb. 2021, www.investopedia.com/terms/c/commoditychannelindex.asp#:~:text=The%20Commodity%20Channel%20Index%20(CCI)%20is%20a%20technical%20indicator%20that,is%20below%20the%20historic%20average.

209. Mitchell, Cory. "Detrended Price Oscillator (DPO) Definition and Uses." *Investopedia*, Investopedia, 9 Mar. 2021, www.investopedia.com/terms/d/detrended-price-oscillator-dpo.asp.

210. Mitchell, Cory. "Downside Tasuki Gap Definition and Example." *Investopedia*, Investopedia, 27 Nov. 2020, www.investopedia.com/terms/d/downside-tasuki-gap.asp.

211. Mitchell, Cory. "Fibonacci Channel Definition and Uses." *Investopedia*, Investopedia, 30 Apr. 2021, www.investopedia.com/terms/f/fibonaccichannel.asp.

212. Mitchell, Cory. "Fibonacci Retracement Levels." *Investopedia*, Investopedia, 29 Apr. 2021, www.investopedia.com/terms/f/fibonacciretracement.asp.

213. Mitchell, Cory. "Gann Angles." *Investopedia*, Investopedia, 14 Oct. 2020, www.investopedia.com/terms/g/gannangles.asp.

214. Mitchell, Cory. "Gann Fans Definition and Uses." *Investopedia*, Investopedia, 2 May 2021, www.investopedia.com/terms/g/gann-fans.asp.

215. Mitchell, Cory. "Harami Cross Definition and Example." *Investopedia*, Investopedia, 29 Aug. 2020, www.investopedia.com/terms/h/haramicross.asp#:~:text=A%20harami%20cross%20is%20a,may%20be%20about%20to%20reverse.

216. Mitchell, Cory. "Heikin-Ashi Technique Definition and Example." *Investopedia*, Investopedia, 16 Feb. 2021, www.investopedia.com/terms/h/heikinashi.asp#:~:text=Renko%20Charts,by%20time%2C%20only%20by%20movement.

217. Mitchell, Cory. "How Traders Use CCI (Commodity Channel Index) to Trade Stock Trends." *Investopedia*, Investopedia, 9 Nov. 2020, www.investopedia.com/articles/active-trading/031914/how-traders-can-utilize-cci-commodity-channel-index-trade-stock-trends.asp.

218. Mitchell, Cory. "How Triple Tops Warn You a Stock's Going to Drop." *Investopedia*, Investopedia, 7 Jan. 2021, www.investopedia.com/terms/t/tripletop.asp.

219. Mitchell, Cory. "Ichimoku Cloud Definition and Uses." *Investopedia*, Investopedia, 30 Apr. 2021, www.investopedia.com/terms/i/ichimoku-cloud.asp.

220. Mitchell, Cory. "Ichimoku Cloud Definition and Uses." *Investopedia*, Investopedia, 30 Apr. 2021, www.investopedia.com/terms/i/ichimoku-cloud.asp.

221. Mitchell, Cory. "Klinger Oscillator Definition." *Investopedia*, Investopedia, 28 Aug. 2020, www.investopedia.com/terms/k/klingeroscillator.asp#:~:text=The%20Klinger%20oscillator%20was%20developed,the%20result%20into%20an%20oscillator.

222. Mitchell, Cory. "Money Flow Index - MFI Definition and Uses." *Investopedia*, Investopedia, 28 Aug. 2020, www.investopedia.com/terms/m/mfi.asp.

223. Mitchell, Cory. "Percentage Price Oscillator (PPO) Definition." *Investopedia*, Investopedia, 6 May 2021, www.investopedia.com/terms/p/ppo.asp.

224. Mitchell, Cory. "Reversal." *Investopedia*, Investopedia, 5 Jan. 2021, www.investopedia.com/terms/r/reversal.asp.

225. Mitchell, Cory. "Spinning Top Candlestick." *Investopedia*, Investopedia, 3 Feb. 2021, www.investopedia.com/terms/s/spinning-top.asp.

226. Mitchell, Cory. "Trailing Stop Definition and Uses." *Investopedia*, Investopedia, 7 May 2021, www.investopedia.com/terms/t/trailingstop.asp.

227. Mitchell, Cory. "Triangle Chart Patterns and Day Trading Strategies." *The Balance*, 12 Sept. 2020, www.thebalance.com/triangle-chart-patterns-and-day-trading-strategies-4111224.

228. Mitchell, Cory. "True Strength Index (TSI) Definition." *Investopedia*, Investopedia, 12 May 2021, www.investopedia.com/terms/t/tsi.asp.

229. Mitchell, Cory. "Ultimate Oscillator Definition and Strategies." *Investopedia*, Investopedia, 28 Aug. 2020, www.investopedia.com/terms/u/ultimateoscillator.asp.

230. Mitchell, Cory. "Upside Gap Two Crows Definition and Example." *Investopedia*, Investopedia, 2 Feb. 2021, www.investopedia.com/terms/u/upside-gap-two-crows.asp.

231. modelinvesting.com, Model Investing -. "The Risk-Return Trade-Off." *Model Investing*, 19 Oct. 2018, modelinvesting.com/articles/the-risk-return-trade-off/.

232. Mohr, Melanie. "Crypto Trends of 2020." *Medium*, The Capital, 18 Jan. 2020, medium.com/the-capital/crypto-trends-of-2020-8ba2fe5da60d.

233. "Momentum Indicators - Overview, Advantages, Examples." *Corporate Finance Institute*, corporatefinanceinstitute.com/resources/knowledge/trading-investing/momentum-indicators/.

234. "Money Flow Index (MFI)." *Money Flow Index (MFI) [ChartSchool]*, school.stockcharts.com/doku.php?id=technical_indicators%3Amoney_flow_index_mfi.

235. "Morning Doji Star." *CandleScanner*, www.candlescanner.com/candlestick-patterns/morning-doji-star/#:~:text=The%20Morning%20Doji%20Star%20is,similar%20to%20the%20Morning%20Star.&text=It%20happens%20that%20two%20first,resistance%20zone%20or%20a%20trendline.

236. "The Most Powerful Crypto Trading Bot." *Cryptohopper*, www.cryptohopper.com/.

237. "Moving Average." *Trend Indicators - MetaTrader 5 Help*, www.metatrader5.com/en/terminal/help/indicators/trend_indicators/ma#:~:text=There%20are%20four%20different%20types,volume%20or%20any%20other%20indicators.

238. Murphy, Casey. "Introduction to the Parabolic SAR." *Investopedia*, Investopedia, 5 Apr. 2021, www.investopedia.com/trading/introduction-to-parabolic-sar/.

239. Murphy, Casey. "What Is a Pitchfork Indicator & How Do I Use It?" *Investopedia*, Investopedia, 2 Mar. 2021, www.investopedia.com/ask/answers/05/andrewpitchfork.asp.

240. "Nature, The Golden Ratio, and Fibonacci Too ..." *Math Is Fun*, www.mathsisfun.com/numbers/nature-golden-ratio-fibonacci.html.

241. "The Numbers of Nature: the Fibonacci Sequence." *Eniscuola*, 5 July 2016, www.eniscuola.net/en/2016/06/27/the-numbers-of-nature-the-fibonacci-sequence/.

242. Object], [object. "The Best Crypto Trading Bots On the Market." *TokenTax*, tokentax.co/blog/best-crypto-trading-bot/.

243. "Online Crypto Currency Volatility Calculator." *Crypto Volatility*, www.cryptovolatility.net/'.

244. Online, FE. "Fundamental or Technical Analysis: Which Is Better?" *The Financial Express*, The Financial Express, 30 July 2019, www.financialexpress.com/market/fundamental-or-technical-analysis-which-is-better/1659945/#:~:text=Fundamental%20analysis%20is%20more%20theoretical%20because%20it%20seeks%20to%20determine,at%20times%2C%20to%20be%20irrational.

245. "Oscillators - Technical Indicators - Education." *TradingView*, www.tradingview.com/education/oscillator/.

246. "Parabolic SAR - Overview, How It Works, and How to Calculate." *Corporate Finance Institute*, 1 Apr. 2019, corporatefinanceinstitute.com/resources/knowledge/trading-investing/parabolic-sar/.

247. "Parabolic SAR - Overview, How It Works, and How to Calculate." *Corporate Finance Institute*, 1 Apr. 2019, corporatefinanceinstitute.com/resources/knowledge/trading-investing/parabolic-sar/.

248. Parker, Tim. "Has High Frequency Trading Ruined the Stock Market for the Rest of Us?" *Investopedia*, Investopedia, 3 May 2021, www.investopedia.com/financial-edge/0113/has-high-frequency-trading-ruined-the-stock-market-for-the-rest-of-us.aspx#:~:text=By%20purchasing%20at%20the%20bid,multiplied%20over%20millions%20of%20shares.

249. Parker, Tim. "Has High Frequency Trading Ruined the Stock Market for the Rest of Us?" *Investopedia*, Investopedia, 3 May 2021, www.investopedia.com/financial-edge/0113/has-high-frequency-trading-ruined-the-stock-market-for-the-rest-of-us.aspx#:~:text=By%20purchasing%20at%20the%20bid,multiplied%20over%20millions%20of%20shares.

250. Pasternak, Melvin. "The Rectangle Formation." *Investopedia*, Investopedia, 28 Aug. 2020, www.investopedia.com/articles/trading/08/rectangle-formation.asp.

251. "Patterns Dictionary." *CandleScanner*, www.candlescanner.com/patterns-dictionary/.

252. Pechman, Marcel. "3 On-Chain Metrics Crypto Investors Use to Track Bitcoin Network Activity." *Cointelegraph*, Cointelegraph, 11 June 2020, cointelegraph.com/news/3-on-chain-metrics-crypto-investors-use-to-track-bitcoin-network-activity.

253. Pedro Febrero janvier 31, 2020, et al. "How Does Risk and Reward Work in Cryptocurrency?" *Coin Rivet*, 31 Jan. 2020, coinrivet.com/fr/how-does-risk-and-reward-work-in-cryptocurrency/#:~:text=According%20to%20Investopedia%2C%20%E2%80%9Cthe%20risk,undertake%20to%20earn%20these%20returns.

254. Pedro Febrero janvier 31, 2020, et al. "How Does Risk and Reward Work in Cryptocurrency?" *Coin Rivet*, 31 Jan. 2020, coinrivet.com/fr/how-does-risk-and-reward-work-in-cryptocurrency/#:~:text=According%20to%20Investopedia%2C%20%E2%80%9Cthe%20risk,undertake%20to%20earn%20these%20returns.

255. "Percentage Price Oscillator." *Percentage Price Oscillator [ChartSchool]*, school.stockcharts.com/doku.php?id=technical_indicators%3Aprice_oscillators_ppo.

256. "Percentage Volume Oscillator." *Percentage Volume Oscillator [ChartSchool]*, school.stockcharts.com/doku.php?id=technical_indicators%3Apercentage_volume_oscillator_pvo.

257. Picardo, Elvis. "Four Big Risks of Algorithmic High-Frequency Trading." *Investopedia*, Investopedia, 28 Aug. 2020, www.investopedia.com/articles/markets/012716/four-big-risks-algorithmic-highfrequency-trading.asp.

258. Pines, Lawrence. "Doji Formations: Learn How to Interpret Them to Help Trading Strategies." *Commodity.com*, 24 Feb. 2021, commodity.com/technical-analysis/doji/.

259. Pines, Lawrence. "How Traders Use The Detrended Price Oscillator To Suss Out Underlying Price Movements." *Commodity.com*, 23 Feb. 2021, commodity.com/technical-analysis/detrended-price-oscillator/.

260. Posted on January 14, 2019 by Angel - Technical Analysis. "What Are Gann Angles and How Do You Use Them to Trade?" *Bullish Bears Trading: Stocks, Options & Futures + Free Stock Market Courses*, 23 Mar. 2021, bullishbears.com/gann-angles/.

261. "Professional Crypto Trading Bot Platform & API." *CryptoHero*, 10 May 2021, cryptohero.ai/.

262. "The Psychology of Money." *HCPLive*, www.hcplive.com/view/the-psychology-of-money.

263. "r/CryptoCurrency - DOGECOIN Has an Unlimited Supply, Can We Talk about This More?" *Reddit*, www.reddit.com/r/CryptoCurrency/comments/lcklfe/dogecoin_has_an_unlimited_supply_can_we_talk/.

264. Rayner. "How to Use Trailing Stop Loss (5 Powerful Techniques That Work)." *TradingwithRayner*, Rayner Teo, 28 Oct. 2020, www.tradingwithrayner.com/trailing-stop-loss/.

265. Rayner. "The Monster Guide to Candlestick Patterns." *TradingWithRayner*, Rayner Teo, 2 Oct. 2020, www.tradingwithrayner.com/candlestick-patterns/.

266. Reiff, Nathan. "Cryptocurrency 'Burning': Can It Manage Inflation?" *Investopedia*, Investopedia, 24 Nov. 2020, www.investopedia.com/tech/cryptocurrency-burning-can-it-manage-inflation/.

267. Reiff, Nathan. "How to Identify the Next Big Cryptocurrency." *Investopedia*, Investopedia, 28 Aug. 2020, www.investopedia.com/news/how-identify-next-big-cryptocurrency/.

268. Richard Snow, Laura Wagg. "Pennant Patterns: Trading Bearish & Bullish Pennants." *DailyFX*, www.dailyfx.com/education/technical-analysis-chart-patterns/pennant-pattern.html.

269. Robert W. Colby, CMT. *Latest Edition, Completely Revised Encyclopedia of Technical Market Indicators, Second Edition, by Robert W. Colby, CMT, Featuring the Best, Top-Performing Market Timing Methods, Models, Trading Systems, Technical Analysis, and Indicators for Trading and Investing*, www.robertwcolby.com/booksalespromo.html.

270. Rolf, and Elxtrx. "5 Best Trading Oscillator Indicators to Find Market Entries -." *Tradeciety Online Trading*, 20 Apr. 2021, tradeciety.com/5-best-trading-oscillator-indicators-to-find-market-entries/.

271. Rosenberg, Eric, and Goodwill says: "Technical Analysis vs. Fundamental Analysis: What Are the Differences?" *Investor Junkie*, 25 Mar. 2021, investorjunkie.com/investing/what-is-technical-analysis-vs-fundamental-analysis/.

272. "Run Crypto Market Making Bots and Join Liquidity Mining." *Hummingbot*, hummingbot.io/.

273. Ryan, Jake. "Crypto Fundamental Analysis-9 Metrics, Indicators & Ratios, Part II."
     Tradecraft Capital, Tradecraft Capital, 24 Aug. 2019,
     www.tradecraft.capital/blog/2019/08/08/crypto-fundamental-analysis%E2%80%8A-
     %E2%80%8A9-metrics-indicators-ratios-part-ii.

274. Ryan, Jake. "Cryptoasset Fundamental Analysis-7 Indicators & Ratios to Watch."
     Medium, Medium, 21 Dec. 2020, tradecraftjake.medium.com/cryptoasset-fundamental-
     analysis-7-indicators-ratios-to-watch-470c56076c2e.

275. Samuelsson. "Does Algorithmic Trading Work? (With Steps to Make It Work For
     You!)." *THE ROBUST TRADER*, 13 Apr. 2021, therobusttrader.com/does-algorithmic-
     trading-
     work/#:~:text=Yes%2C%20algorithmic%20trading%20does%20work,rules%20are%2
     0quantifiable%20and%20retestable.

276. Samuelsson. "Is Algorithmic Trading Hard? - Is Algo Trading Difficult?" *THE
     ROBUST TRADER*, 13 Apr. 2021, therobusttrader.com/is-algorithmic-trading-hard/.

277. Samuelsson. "Volume Indicators: How to Use Volume in Trading (List)." *THE
     ROBUST TRADER*, 13 Apr. 2021, therobusttrader.com/volume-indicators-volume-
     trading/.

278. SatoshiLabs. "Bitcoin Has No Problem with Deflation. Fiat Does." *Medium*, Trezor
     Blog, 18 June 2020, blog.trezor.io/bitcoin-has-no-problem-with-deflation-fiat-does-
     395468654820.

279. says:, Deepti Waghmare. "High-Frequency Trading Comes to Cryptocurrency." *The
     FinReg Blog*, 2 June 2020, sites.law.duke.edu/thefinregblog/2019/04/24/high-frequency-
     trading-comes-to-cryptocurrency/.

280. "Schiff Pitchfork." *TradingView*,
     www.tradingview.com/support/solutions/43000518140-schiff-pitchfork/.

281. "Schiff Pitchfork." *Visit the Main Page*, www.multicharts.com/trading-
     software/index.php/Schiff_Pitchfork.

282. "School." *TradingView*, www.tradingview.com/ideas/school/.

283. Scott, Gordon. "Trading Psychology Definition." *Investopedia*, Investopedia, 16 Sept.
     2020, www.investopedia.com/terms/t/trading-psychology.asp.

284. Sean, and Pat Crawley. "How To Use The Awesome Oscillator." *Warrior Trading*, 5
     Mar. 2020, www.warriortrading.com/awesome-
     oscillator/#:~:text=The%20simplest%20way%20to%20interpret,is%20indicative%20of
     %20bearish%20momentum.

285. Sean, and Pat Crawley. "Point and *(tradingview.com)* Figure Chart Explained for
     Beginners." *Warrior Trading*, 7 Aug. 2020, www.warriortrading.com/point-and-figure-
     chart/.

286. Sean, et al. "How to Trade the Three Line Strike Candlestick Pattern." *Warrior
     Trading*, 31 Mar. 2020, www.warriortrading.com/three-line-strike/.

287. Segal, Troy. "Understanding Momentum Indicators and RSI." *Investopedia*,
     Investopedia, 1 May 2021, www.investopedia.com/investing/momentum-and-relative-
     strength-index/.

288. Seth, Shobhit. "Basics of Algorithmic Trading: Concepts and Examples." *Investopedia*,
     Investopedia, 5 May 2021, www.investopedia.com/articles/active-
     trading/101014/basics-algorithmic-trading-concepts-and-examples.asp.

289. Seth, Shobhit. "Technical Analysis Strategies for Beginners." *Investopedia*, Investopedia,
     29 Apr. 2021, www.investopedia.com/articles/active-trading/102914/technical-analysis-
     strategies-beginners.asp.

290. Seth, Shobhit. "The World of High-Frequency Algorithmic Trading." *Investopedia*, Investopedia, 29 Aug. 2020, www.investopedia.com/articles/investing/091615/world-high-frequency-algorithmic-trading.asp.

291. Sinclair, Sebastian. "Crypto Trading 101: Stochastic Oscillators and Price Momentum." *CoinDesk*, CoinDesk, 7 Aug. 2018, www.coindesk.com/crypto-trading-101-stochastic-oscillators-and-price-momentum.

292. "Smart Crypto Investing." *Stacked*, stackedinvest.com/.

293. "Smart Trading Terminal and Crypto Trading Bots." *3Commas*, 3commas.io/.

294. *SMI Ergodic Indicator and Oscillator*, www.tc2000.com/Help/Content/Indicators/SMI%20Ergodic%20Indicator%20and%20Oscillator.htm.

295. "SMI Ergodic Oscillator - Indicators and Signals." *TradingView*, www.tradingview.com/scripts/ergodic/.

296. *SMI Ergodic Oscillator*, www.motivewave.com/studies/smi_ergodic_oscillator.htm.

297. Smigel, Leo. "Algorithmic Trading: Is It Worth It?" *Analyzing Alpha*, Analyzing Alpha, 17 Oct. 2019, analyzingalpha.com/algorithmic-trading-is-it-worth-it.

298. Smith, Tim. "Upside Tasuki Gap." *Investopedia*, Investopedia, 15 May 2021, www.investopedia.com/terms/u/upside-tasuki-gap.asp.

299. Snow, Richard. "3 Triangle Patterns Every Forex Trader Should Know." *DailyFX*, www.dailyfx.com/education/technical-analysis-chart-patterns/triangle-pattern.html.

300. Spaulding, William C. "An Overview of Chart Types Used in Technical Analysis." *An Overview Of Chart Types Used In Technical Analysis: Line Charts, Bar Charts, Candlestick Charts, and Point-and-(tradingview.com) Figure Charts*, thismatter.com/money/technical-analysis/chart-types.htm.

301. "Spinning Top Candlestick: a Trader's Guide." *IG*, www.ig.com/en/trading-strategies/spinning-top-candlestick--a-trader-s-guide-200203#:~:text=What%20does%20a%20spinning%20top,reversal%20is%20about%20to%20occur.

302. Sraders, Anne. "What Is Technical Analysis? Definition, Basics and Examples." *TheStreet*, TheStreet, 29 May 2019, www.thestreet.com/investing/technical-analysis-14920339.

303. Stably. "How to Build a Simple Bitcoin Trading Algorithm (Part 1/2)." *Medium*, Stably, 20 Mar. 2020, medium.com/stably-blog/how-to-build-a-simple-bitcoin-trading-algorithm-part-1-2-edbb94e1b20e.

304. Staff, Investopedia. "An Introduction to Oscillators." *Investopedia*, Investopedia, 15 Jan. 2021, www.investopedia.com/articles/technical/070301.asp.

305. Staff, Investopedia. "Confirming Price Movements With Volume Oscillators." *Investopedia*, Investopedia, 5 Apr. 2021, www.investopedia.com/articles/technical/02/082702.asp#:~:text=A%20look%20at%20volume%20from,of%20buying%20and%20selling%20activity.&text=A%20volume%20oscillator%20measures%20volume,and%20slow%20volume%20moving%20average.

306. Staff, Investopedia. "Point and *(tradingview.com)* Figure Charting: A Basic Introduction." *Investopedia*, Investopedia, 29 Aug. 2020, www.investopedia.com/articles/technical/03/081303.asp.

307. Staff, Investopedia. "Triangles: A Short Study in Continuation Patterns." *Investopedia*, Investopedia, 22 Jan. 2021, www.investopedia.com/articles/technical/03/091003.asp.

308. "Step-by-Step Guide to Trade the Rounding Bottom Pattern." *Tradingsim*, 8 Aug. 2018, tradingsim.com/blog/rounding-bottom/#:~:text=One%20of%20the%20variations%20of,decrease%20prior%20to%20t

he%20breakout.&text=The%20cup%20and%20handle%20pattern%20is%20essentiall
y%20traded,way%20as%20the%20rounding%20bottom.

309. Stieg, Cory. "Why People Are so Obsessed with Bitcoin: The Psychology of Crypto Explained." *CNBC*, CNBC, 25 Jan. 2021, www.cnbc.com/2021/01/23/why-people-invest-in-bitcoin.html.

310. "Stochastic Oscillator." *Stochastic Oscillator [ChartSchool]*, school.stockcharts.com/doku.php?id=technical_indicators%3Astochastic_oscillator_fast _slow_and_full.

311. StocksToTrade, Tim Bohen From, et al. "Trading Psychology: Guide to Master Your Mind in 7 Steps." *StocksToTrade*, 23 Apr. 2021, stockstotrade.com/trading-psychology/.

312. Superorder.io. "Basics of Market Psychology in Crypto Trading." *Medium*, Superorder, 19 Oct. 2019, medium.com/superorder/basics-of-market-psychology-in-crypto-trading-72f09dbefe8d.

313. Superorder.io. "Basics of Market Psychology in Crypto Trading." *Medium*, Superorder, 19 Oct. 2019, medium.com/superorder/basics-of-market-psychology-in-crypto-trading-72f09dbefe8d.

314. *Supply and Demand: The Market Mechanism*, kr.mnsu.edu/~cu7296vs/supdem.htm.

315. *TC2000 Help Site*, help.tc2000.com/m/69404/l/1220419-smi-ergodic-indicator-and-oscillator.

316. Team, Editorial. "Bitcoin Halving: What Does This Mean and What Will Its Effect Be?" *Finextra Research*, Finextra, 12 May 2020, www.finextra.com/the-long-read/40/bitcoin-halving-what-does-this-mean-and-what-will-its-effect-be.

317. Team, Trading Education. "20 Types Of Technical Indicators Used By Trading Gurus." *Trading Education*, Trading Education, 5 Aug. 2019, trading-education.com/20-technical-indicators-used-by-trading-gurus.

318. Team, Trading Education. "Top 10 Crypto YouTubers To Subscribe To By Number Of Subscribers." *Trading Education*, Trading Education, 7 Oct. 2019, trading-education.com/top-10-crypto-youtubers-to-subscribe-to-by-number-of-subscribers.

319. "Technical Analysis - Beginner's Guide to Technical Charts." *Corporate Finance Institute*, 24 Aug. 2019, corporatefinanceinstitute.com/resources/knowledge/trading-investing/technical-analysis/.

320. "Technical Analysis Charts: Types of Technical Analysis Charts." *Investar Blog*, 9 Dec. 2020, investarindia.com/blog/technical-analysis-charts/.

321. "Technical Analysis Definition." *IG*, www.ig.com/en/glossary-trading-terms/technical-analysis-definition.

322. "Technical Analysis Definitive Guide [2021]." *Warrior Trading*, 14 Apr. 2021, www.warriortrading.com/technical-analysis/.

323. "Technical Analysis for Bitcoin and Other Crypto." *Gemini*, www.gemini.com/cryptopedia/technical-analysis-bitcoin-and-crypto.

324. "Technical Indicators: Barchart.com Education." *Barchart.com*, www.barchart.com/education/technical-indicators/percentage_volume_oscillator.

325. This Trading Life. "What's Your Trading Mantra?" *This Trading Life*, This Trading Life, 31 July 2020, www.thistradinglife.com/post/trading-mantra-mindset.

326. "Three-Line Strike Pattern: Complete Guide [2021]." *PatternsWizard*, 1 Mar. 2021, patternswizard.com/three-line-strike-candlestick-pattern/.

327. "Three-Line Strike Pattern: Complete Guide [2021]." *PatternsWizard*, 1 Mar. 2021, patternswizard.com/three-line-strike-candlestick-pattern/.

328. "Token Burning Mechanisms." *Bitcoin Suisse*, 2 Mar. 2021, www.bitcoinsuisse.com/research/decrypt/token-burning-mechanisms.

329. "Top 4 Awesome Oscillator Day Trading Strategies." *Tradingsim*, 31 Dec. 2020, tradingsim.com/blog/awesome-oscillator/.

330. "Top 7 Technical Analysis Tools." *Investopedia*, Investopedia, 30 Apr. 2021, www.investopedia.com/top-7-technical-analysis-tools-4773275.

331. "Trade-Volume." *Blockchain.com*, www.blockchain.com/charts/trade-volume.

332. "A Trader's Guide to the Detrended Price Oscillator." *IG*, www.ig.com/en/trading-strategies/a-traders-guide-to-the-detrended-price-oscillator-200327.

333. "Trading 101: Volatility Indicators Explained." *Cryptohopper*, www.cryptohopper.com/blog/178-trading-101-volatility-indicators-explained.

334. "Trading Patterns." *Day Trading*, www.daytrading.com/patterns.

335. "Trading Strategies, Signals and Technical Indicators." *TradingView*, www.tradingview.com/scripts/.

336. "TradingView Automated Trading." *TradingView Automated Trading*, trading.wunderbit.co/en/tradingview-automated-trading.

337. "Trend and Continuation Patterns - CME Group." *Futures & Options Trading for Risk Management - CME Group*, www.cmegroup.com/education/courses/technical-analysis/trend-and-continuation-patterns.html.

338. "Triangle Patterns - Technical Analysis." *Corporate Finance Institute*, 26 Apr. 2020, corporatefinanceinstitute.com/resources/knowledge/trading-investing/triangle-patterns/.

339. "True Strength Index: Best Settings for a Day Trading Strategy - DTTW™." *Day Trade The World™*, 28 Apr. 2021, www.daytradetheworld.com/trading-blog/true-strength-index-in-day-trading/.

340. Twiggs, Colin. "Candlestick Chart Patterns: Strongest to Weakest." *Incredible Charts Stock Market Charting Software.*, www.incrediblecharts.com/candlestick_patterns/candlestick-patterns-strongest.php.

341. Twiggs, Colin. "Chande Momentum Oscillator." *Incredible Charts Stock Market Charting Software.*, www.incrediblecharts.com/indicators/chande-momentum-oscillator.php.

342. Twiggs, Colin. "Detrended Price Oscillator." *Incredible Charts Stock Market Charting Software.*, www.incrediblecharts.com/indicators/detrended_price_oscillator.php.

343. Twin, Alexandra. "What Is Volume of Trade?" *Investopedia*, Investopedia, 12 Mar. 2021, www.investopedia.com/terms/v/volumeoftrade.asp.

344. "Ultimate Bitcoin Bot: Become a Smart Crypto Investor." *NapBots*, 27 Apr. 2021, napbots.com/.

345. Venketas, Warren. "The Head and Shoulders Pattern: A Trader's Guide." *DailyFX*, www.dailyfx.com/education/technical-analysis-chart-patterns/head-and-shoulders-pattern.html.

346. Venketas, Warren. "Top 5 Types of Doji Candlesticks." *DailyFX*, www.dailyfx.com/education/candlestick-patterns/types-of-doji.html.

347. Venketas, Warren. "Trading with the Spinning Top Candlestick." *DailyFX*, www.dailyfx.com/education/candlestick-patterns/spinning-top-candle.html.

348. "VO Definition." *Fidelity*, www.fidelity.com/learning-center/trading-investing/technical-analysis/technical-indicator-guide/volume-oscillator.

349. "Walk Me Through a DCF Analysis - Investment Banking Interviews." *Corporate Finance Institute*, 28 Mar. 2021, corporatefinanceinstitute.com/resources/careers/interviews/walk-me-through-a-dcf/.

350. Walk, The Rational. "The Psychology of Money: The Rational Walk." *The Rational Walk* |, 11 Oct. 2020, rationalwalk.com/the-psychology-of-money/.

351. Watkins, Graeme. "6 Types of Technical Analysis Every Forex Trader Should Learn." *Valutrades*, www.valutrades.com/en/blog/6-types-of-technical-analysis-every-forex-trader-should-learn.

352. Watkins, Graeme. "Chart Patterns vs Indicators: What's Best for Technical Analysis?" *Valutrades*, www.valutrades.com/en/blog/chart-patterns-vs-indicators-whats-best-for-technical-analysis.

353. "What Are Bollinger Bands?" *Fidelity*, www.fidelity.com/learning-center/trading-investing/technical-analysis/technical-indicator-guide/bollinger-bands#:~:text=Bollinger%20Bands%20are%20envelopes%20plotted,Period%20and%20Standard%20Deviations%2C%20StdDev.

354. "What Is CCI? - Commodity Channel Index." *Fidelity*, www.fidelity.com/learning-center/trading-investing/technical-analysis/technical-indicator-guide/cci.

355. "What Is Circulating Supply and How Is It Calculated?" *Paybis Blog*, 17 Jan. 2020, paybis.com/blog/what-is-circulating-supply/.

356. "What Is High-Frequency Trading and How Do You Make Money from It?" *The Guardian*, Guardian News and Media, 19 Dec. 2019, www.theguardian.com/business/2019/dec/19/high-frequency-trading-explainer-bank-of-england-breach.

357. "What Is MACD? - Moving Average Convergence/Divergence." *Fidelity*, www.fidelity.com/learning-center/trading-investing/technical-analysis/technical-indicator-guide/macd.

358. "What Is The Ichimoku Cloud?" *Fidelity*, www.fidelity.com/learning-center/trading-investing/technical-analysis/technical-indicator-guide/Ichimoku-Cloud.

359. "What Is The UO - Ultimate Oscillator?" *Fidelity*, www.fidelity.com/learning-center/trading-investing/technical-analysis/technical-indicator-guide/ultimate-oscillator.

360. "What Percentage of Our Lives Are Spent Working?" *Reference*, IAC Publishing, www.reference.com/world-view/percentage-lives-spent-working-599e3f7fb2c88fca#:~:text=About%20one%2Dthird%20or%2030,25%20to%2030%20years%20working.

361. "White Papers Archives." *CoinDesk*, CoinDesk, www.coindesk.com/tag/white-papers.

362. White, Alexandria. "73% Of Americans Rank Their Finances as the No. 1 Stress in Life, According to New Capital One CreditWise Survey." *CNBC*, CNBC, 1 Feb. 2021, www.cnbc.com/select/73-percent-of-americans-rank-finances-as-the-number-one-stress-in-life/.

363. *Whitepapers*, cryptorating.eu/whitepapers/.

364. Wiesflecker, Lukas. "What Is a Coin Burn, and How Does Coin Burning Work?" *Medium*, Coinmonks, 28 Dec. 2020, medium.com/coinmonks/what-is-a-coin-burn-and-how-does-coin-burning-work-c30131f5c4e3.

365. "William Delbert Gann: The Mysterious Trader." *PatternsWizard*, 1 Mar. 2021, patternswizard.com/wd-gann/.

366. Woods, Galen. "5 Day Trader's Tricks to Control Your Emotions." *Trading Setups Review*, 13 Sept. 2016, www.tradingsetupsreview.com/5-day-traders-tricks-control-emotions/.

367. Www.optimusfutures.com/facebook. "Does Intuition and Gut Feeling Play a Role in Trading?" *Futures Day Trading Strategies*, 6 June 2018, optimusfutures.com/tradeblog/archives/does-intuition-and-gut-feeling-play-a-role-in-trading#:~:text=Intuition%20does%20not%20only%20play,but%20it%20goes%20much%20deeper.&text=This%20is%20why%20having%20a,but%20based%20on%20your%20analysis.

368. Zucchi, Kristina. "How to Avoid Emotional Investing." *Investopedia*, Investopedia, 24 Mar. 2021, www.investopedia.com/articles/basics/10/how-to-avoid-emotional-investing.asp.

369. "_checkonchain." *_checkonchain On-Chain Analysis Suite*, checkonchain.com/.

FIGURE GUIDE

BONUS SECTION: BLOCKCHAIN

We've previously touched on the idea of the blockchain; it can simply be described as a new type of database, created in order to transfer cryptocurrency without a centralized middleman. You don't need to be an expert on everything blockchain, but every action you take in relation to anything crypto is most likely founded on blockchain networks. Therefore, we'll cover it in the most understandable way possible. The goal, at least initially, should be to understand the concepts at hand and be able to use the terms that surround blockchain.

BLOCKCHAIN IN THEORY: THE JEWELRY THIEF.

We will now take a moment to understand how the decentralization of blockchain and the accompanying networks allows for ultra-secure transactions and safe storage of assets.

Imagine this: Two billionaires purchase $100 million worth of valuable diamonds. Both take pride in their security, although their methods are very different. Billionaire #1 keeps his jewels in an vault in a location surrounded by security cameras, guards, and blast-proof walls. Billionaire #2 moves her jewels constantly to new locations based on a randomized system; any location the jewels end up belongs to other people in far-off places. The people holding the jewels, not her, nor anyone knows where the jewels are at any given time; to access them she must use a backup code that only she knows. Even if the jewels were found, they're protected by mathematical equations that are extremely difficult to solve; doing so would take years for even the brightest minds. Billionaire #1 soon discovers his jewels are missing. Why? Who knows? Maybe the security systems were hacked, maybe a guard or other insiders helped the intruder gain access, maybe the intruder conned his way in, maybe the entire security force conspired against the billionaire to steal his jewels.

This, in essence, is centralization versus decentralization. While real-life examples are certainly prone to the unique situation and the mentioned example certainly isn't a realistic situation, the basis is sound. Centralization be attacked from a variety of angles and is prone to human error and malevolence. Decentralization removes the opportunity for human error (assuming your seed phrase stays private. If you're hacked because someone used your seed phrase, that's a personal error, not an issue with the larger network. It's also quite easy to keep your seed phrase safe), and provides an entire network that relies on many different computers to keep data secure. Additionally, centralized financial services always reserve the right to stop providing their services to you and your money; hence, fees can be raised, companies can go under, databases can be hacked, etc. Decentralized networks rely on an algorithm; this algorithm cannot be changed once put into place and hence, so to speak, the rules of the game cannot be changed. The same cannot be said for centralization. That, in essence, is the core concept of blockchain; we shall now move on the practical, technical side of blockchains.

BLOCKCHAIN: BROKEN DOWN

Blockchain, in its most basic form, can be thought of as storing data in literal chains of blocks. Let's walk through how exactly blocks and chains come into play.

- Each block will store digital information, such as the time, date, amount, etc. of transactions.
- The block will also store who participated in a transaction by using your "digital key," which is a string of numbers and letters that you receive every time you open a wallet.
- Blocks cannot operate on their own. Blocks need verification from other computers, aka "nodes" in the network.

Nodes

You will hear "node" and "nodes thrown around all the time. In the crypto space, a node is a computer that connects to a cryptocurrency network. Bitcoin has tens of thousands of nodes, while other cryptocurrencies may have more or less.

- The other nodes will validate the information of one block. Once they validate the data, and if everything looks good, the block and the data it carries will be stored in the public ledger.
- The public ledger is a database that records every single approved transaction ever made on the network. For example, the Bitcoin blockchain has its own public ledger.
- Each block in the ledger is linked to the block that came before it and the block that came after it. Hence, the links the blocks form create a chain-like pattern and a blockchain is formed.

Summary: The **block** represents digital information, and the **chain** represents how that data is stored in the database.

So, to recap our earlier definition, blockchain is a new type of database. We now know what the block and the chain represent, but the last part of the equation only touched upon is the public ledger.

Blockchain is a DLT technology. DLT stands for Distributed Ledger Technology. DLT technology is revolutionary because it solves the issue of trust. For example, if someone runs a popular transactional network, how do we know that they won't just take some of the money for themselves? Or, if we keep our money with their network, how do we know they won't raise fees, shut our account down, or go bankrupt? Really, although it's unlikely, we don't. DLT technology solves this problem by being distributed. All participants (digital participants, meaning computers) in the network have a copy of the ledger, which records every single transaction, along with the amount and a timestamp. Here, I ask you to visit either of the following webpages:

https://www.blockchain.com/btc/unconfirmed-transactions

https://etherscan.io/

With these two links, you can explore the public ledger of Bitcoin and Ethereum. You'll be able to see the amount of the transaction, the time at which the transaction took place, and the two addresses involved. Public ledgers and DLT technologies lie at the core of blockchain and allow cryptocurrencies to operate as they do.

BLOCKCHAIN: ORIGINS

The following is a brief history of blockchain:

- In 1991, a cryptographically secured chain of blocks was conceptualized for the first time.
- Nearly a decade later, in 2000, Stegan Knost published his theory on cryptography secured chains, as well as ideas for practical implementation.
- 8 years after that, Satoshi Nakamoto released a white paper (a white paper is a thorough report and guide) that established a model for a blockchain, and, in 2009 Nakamoto implemented the first blockchain, which was used as the public ledger for transactions made with the cryptocurrency he developed, called Bitcoin.
- Finally, in 2014, use cases (use cases are specific situations in which a product or service could potentially be used) for blockchain and blockchain networks were developed outside of cryptocurrency, hence opening up the possibilities of Bitcoin to the wider world.

BLOCKCHAIN Q&A

Q: Are there multiple types of blockchains?

A: Yes. There are four main types of blockchains: public, consortium, hybrid, and private. All are used in varying degrees; the single most common are public blockchains. Anyone with a computer and an internet connection has access to a public blockchain.

Q: Is blockchain safe?

A: Yes. Blockchain is very secure, since each transaction must get approved by many separate nodes (nodes are computers in the network).

Q: How would you explain blockchain to a 5-year-old?

A: Blockchain is a tool that lets many different people safely pass around valuable information without giving someone else control.

Q: Have blockchain networks ever been hacked?

A: To hack a blockchain network, a 51% attack would need to be carried out (for a full definition, please refer to the definition section.) A 51% attack involves a group of attackers, called miners, having enough computers and raw processing power to essentially hijack the network by controlling the majority share needed to validate transactions. If this happens, they can use their control to alter transactions. This type of attack has never been successfully carried out and a blockchain network has yet to be hacked.

However, that said, the exchanges on which transactions are carried out, such as Coinbase, Binance, and Kraken, are much easier to hack. Hacks on exchanges have been successfully carried out many times; in fact, in 2019, 12 crypto exchanges were hacked, and 510,000 user logins were stolen, along with $292,665,886 worth of crypto. So, ironically enough, the core issue that blockchain fights against, centralization, is the very reason crypto attacks can and have happen.

Q: Can anyone start a blockchain?

A: Technically, yes. Anyone can start a blockchain and create their own coin, although it does take more than a bit of coding experience. Some websites even offer to do it for you, although such services are usually quite expensive. Here are a few sites that have offered this service:

https://dev.cryptolife.net/
https://www.walletbuilders.com/

IMAGE CREDIT

[i] Created by Author

[ii] Image credit: created through TradingView (tradingview.com)

[iii] Image credit: created through TradingView (tradingview.com)

[iv] Image credit: created through TradingView (tradingview.com)

[v] Image credit: created through TradingView (tradingview.com)

[vi] Image Credit: TradingView (tradingview.com)

[vii] Image credit: created through TradingView (tradingview.com)

[vii] Huillet, Marie. "Total Value Locked in DeFi Marks New All Time High Close to $40B." *Cointelegraph*, 10 Feb 2021, cointelegraph.com/news/total-value-locked-in-defi-marks-new-all-time-high-close-to-40b.

[ix] Image Credit: TradingView (tradingview.com)

[x] Image credit: created through TradingView (tradingview.com)

[xi] Image credit: created through TradingView (tradingview.com)

[xii] Image credit: created through TradingView (tradingview.com)

[xiii] Image credit: created through TradingView (tradingview.com)

[xiv] Image credit: created through TradingView (tradingview.com)

[xv] Image credit: created through TradingView (tradingview.com)

[xvi] Image credit: created through TradingView (tradingview.com)

[xvii] Image credit: created through TradingView (tradingview.com)

[xviii] Image Credit: TradingView (tradingview.com)

[xix] Image credit: created through TradingView (tradingview.com)

[xx] Image credit: created through TradingView (tradingview.com)

[xxi] Image credit: created through TradingView (tradingview.com)

[xxii] Image credit: created through TradingView (tradingview.com)

[xxiii] Image credit: created through TradingView (tradingview.com)

[xxiv] Image credit: created through TradingView (tradingview.com)

[xxv] Image credit: created through TradingView (tradingview.com)

[xxvi] Image credit: created through TradingView (tradingview.com)

[xxvii] Image credit: created through TradingView (tradingview.com)

[xxviii] Image credit: created through TradingView (tradingview.com)

[xxix] Image credit: created through TradingView (tradingview.com)

[xxx] Image credit: created through TradingView (tradingview.com)

[xxxi] Image credit: created through TradingView (tradingview.com)

[xxxii] Image credit: created through TradingView (tradingview.com)

[xxxiii] Image credit: created through TradingView (tradingview.com)

[xxxiv] Image credit: created through TradingView (tradingview.com)

[xxxv] Image credit: created through TradingView (tradingview.com)

[xxxvi] Image credit: created through TradingView (tradingview.com)

[xxxvii] Image credit: created through TradingView (tradingview.com)

[xxxviii] Image credit: created through TradingView (tradingview.com)

[xxxix] Image credit: created through TradingView (tradingview.com)

[xl] Image credit: created through TradingView (tradingview.com)

[xli] Image credit: created through TradingView (tradingview.com)

[xlii] Image credit: created through TradingView (tradingview.com)

[xliii] Image credit: created through TradingView (tradingview.com)

[xliv] Image credit: created through TradingView (tradingview.com)

[xlv] Image credit: created through TradingView (tradingview.com)

[xlvi] Image credit: created through TradingView (tradingview.com)

[xlvii] Image credit: created through TradingView (tradingview.com)

[xlviii] Image credit: created through TradingView (tradingview.com)

[xlix] Image credit: created through TradingView (tradingview.com)

[l] Image credit: created through TradingView (tradingview.com)

[li] Image credit: created through TradingView (tradingview.com)

[lii] Image credit: created through TradingView (tradingview.com)

[liii] Image credit: created through TradingView (tradingview.com)

[liv] Image credit: created through TradingView (tradingview.com)

[lv] Image credit: created through TradingView (tradingview.com)

[lvi] Image credit: created through TradingView (tradingview.com)

[lvii] Image credit: created through TradingView (tradingview.com)

[lviii] Image credit: created through TradingView (tradingview.com)

[lix] Image credit: created through TradingView (tradingview.com)

[lx] Image credit: created through TradingView (tradingview.com)

[lxi] Image credit: created through TradingView (tradingview.com)

[lxii] Image credit: created through TradingView (tradingview.com)

[lxiii] Image credit: created through TradingView (tradingview.com)

[lxiv] Image credit: created through TradingView (tradingview.com)

[lxv] Image credit: created through TradingView (tradingview.com)

[lxvi] Image credit: created through TradingView (tradingview.com)

[lxvii] Image credit: created through TradingView (tradingview.com)

[lxviii] Image credit: created through TradingView (tradingview.com)

[lxix] Image credit: created through TradingView (tradingview.com)

[lxx] Image credit: created through TradingView (tradingview.com)

[lxxi] Image credit: created through TradingView (tradingview.com)

[lxxii] Image credit: created through TradingView (tradingview.com)

[lxxiii] Image credit: created through TradingView (tradingview.com)

[lxxiv] Image credit: created through TradingView (tradingview.com)

[lxxv] Image credit: created through TradingView (tradingview.com)

[lxxvi] Image credit: created through TradingView (tradingview.com)

[lxxvii] Image credit: created through TradingView (tradingview.com)

[lxxviii] Image credit: created through TradingView (tradingview.com)

[lxxix] Image credit: created through TradingView (tradingview.com)

[lxxx] Image credit: created through TradingView (tradingview.com)

[lxxxi] Image credit: created through TradingView (tradingview.com)

[lxxxii] Image credit: created through TradingView (tradingview.com)

[lxxxiii] Image credit: created through TradingView (tradingview.com)

[lxxxiv] Image credit: created through TradingView (tradingview.com)

[lxxxv] Image credit: created through TradingView (tradingview.com)

[lxxxvi] Image credit: created through TradingView (tradingview.com)

[lxxxvii] Image credit: created through TradingView (tradingview.com)

[lxxxviii] Image credit: created through TradingView (tradingview.com)

[lxxxix] Image credit: created through TradingView (tradingview.com)

[xc] Image credit: created through TradingView (tradingview.com)

[xci] Image credit: created through TradingView (tradingview.com)

[xcii] Image credit: created through TradingView (tradingview.com)

[xciii] Image credit: created through TradingView (tradingview.com)

[xciv] Image credit: created through TradingView (tradingview.com)

[xcv] Image credit: created through TradingView (tradingview.com)

[xcvi] Image credit: created through TradingView (tradingview.com)

[xcvii] Image credit: created through TradingView (tradingview.com)

[xcviii] Image credit: created through TradingView (tradingview.com)

[xcix] Image credit: created through TradingView (tradingview.com)

[c] Image credit: created through TradingView (tradingview.com)

[ci] Image credit: created through TradingView (tradingview.com)

[cii] Image credit: created through TradingView (tradingview.com)

[ciii] Image credit: created through TradingView (tradingview.com)

[civ] Image credit: created through TradingView (tradingview.com)

[cv] Image credit: created through TradingView (tradingview.com)

[cvi] Image credit: created through TradingView (tradingview.com)

[cvii] Image credit: created through TradingView (tradingview.com)

[cviii] Image credit: created through TradingView (tradingview.com)

[cix] Image credit: created through TradingView (tradingview.com)

[cx] Image credit: created through TradingView (tradingview.com)

[cxi] Image credit: created through TradingView (tradingview.com)

[cxii] Image credit: created through TradingView (tradingview.com)

[cxiii] Image credit: created through TradingView (tradingview.com)

[cxiv] Image credit: created through TradingView (tradingview.com)

[cxv] Image credit: created through TradingView (tradingview.com)

[cxvi] Image credit: created through TradingView (tradingview.com)

[cxvii] Image credit: created through TradingView (tradingview.com)

[cxviii] Image credit: created through TradingView (tradingview.com)

[cxix] Image credit: created through TradingView (tradingview.com)

[cxx] Image credit: created through TradingView (tradingview.com)

[cxxi] Image credit: created through TradingView (tradingview.com)

[cxxii] Image credit: created through TradingView (tradingview.com)

[cxxiii] Image credit: created through TradingView (tradingview.com)

[cxxiv] Image credit: created through TradingView (tradingview.com)

[cxxv] Image credit: created through TradingView (tradingview.com)

[cxxvi] Image credit: created through TradingView (tradingview.com)

[cxxvii] Image credit: created through TradingView (tradingview.com)

[cxxviii] Image credit: created through TradingView (tradingview.com)

[cxxix] Image credit: created through TradingView (tradingview.com)

[cxxx] Image credit: created through TradingView (tradingview.com)

[cxxxi] Image credit: created through TradingView (tradingview.com)

[cxxxii] Image credit: created through TradingView (tradingview.com)

[cxxxiii] Image credit: created through TradingView (tradingview.com)

[cxxxiv] Image credit: created through TradingView (tradingview.com)

[cxxxv] Image credit: created through TradingView (tradingview.com

[cxxxvi] Licensed under a Creative Commons Attribution-Share Alike 4.0 International License

[cxxxvii] Licensed under a Creative Commons Attribution-Share Alike 4.0 International License

[cxxxviii] Image credit: created through TradingView (tradingview.com)

[cxxxix] Image credit: created through TradingView (tradingview.com)

[cxl] Image credit: created through TradingView (tradingview.com)

[cxli] Image credit: created through TradingView (tradingview.com)

[cxlii] Image credit: created through TradingView (tradingview.com)

[cxliii] Image credit: created through TradingView (tradingview.com)

[cxliv] Image credit: created through TradingView (tradingview.com)

[cxlv] Image credit: created through TradingView (tradingview.com)

[cxlvi] Image credit: created through TradingView (tradingview.com)

[cxlvii] Image credit: created through TradingView (tradingview.com)

[cxlviii] Image credit: created through TradingView (tradingview.com)

[cxlix] Image credit: created through TradingView (tradingview.com)

[cl] Image credit: created through TradingView (tradingview.com)

[cli] Image credit: created through TradingView (tradingview.com)

[clii] Image credit: created through TradingView (tradingview.com)

[cliii] Image credit: created through TradingView (tradingview.com)

[cliv] Image credit: created through TradingView (tradingview.com)

[clv] Image credit: created through TradingView (tradingview.com)

[clvi] Image credit: created through TradingView (tradingview.com)

[clvii] Image credit: created through TradingView (tradingview.com)

[clviii] Image credit: created through TradingView (tradingview.com)

[clix] Image credit: created through TradingView (tradingview.com)

[clx] Image credit: created through TradingView (tradingview.com)

[clxi] Image credit: created through TradingView (tradingview.com)

[clxii] Image credit: created through TradingView (tradingview.com)

[clxiii] Image credit: created through TradingView (tradingview.com)

[clxiv] Image credit: created through TradingView (tradingview.com)

[clxv] Image credit: created through TradingView (tradingview.com)

[clxvi] Image credit: created through TradingView (tradingview.com)

[clxvii] Image credit: created through TradingView (tradingview.com)

[clxviii] Image credit: created through TradingView (tradingview.com)

[clxix] Image credit: created through TradingView (tradingview.com)

[clxx] Superorder.io. (2019, October 19). Basics of market psychology in Crypto Trading. Retrieved May 15, 2021, from https://medium.com/superorder/basics-of-market-psychology-in-crypto-trading-72f09dbefe8d

[clxxi] Image Credit: Original Image.

[clxxii] R, Rajandran. "7 Things a Trader Should Understand to Do Proper Backtesting." *Marketcalls*, 24 Mar. 2016, www.marketcalls.in/trading-lessons/7-things-a-trader-should-understand-to-do-proper-backtesting.html.

Hi! Please consider joining the School of Coin email list or following @sapereaudepublishing on Instagram for updates on new books. We appreciate your support.

SAPERE AUDE.

CPSIA information can be obtained
at www.ICGtesting.com
Printed in the USA
LVHW072311050122
707923LV00022B/1467